MILNER CRAFT SERIES

Craft from Recycled Materials

DIANA CROSS

SALLY MILNER PUBLISHING

First published in 1993 by
Sally Milner Publishing Pty Ltd
558 Darling Street
Rozelle NSW 2039 Australia

Design by Gatya Kelly, Doric Order
Illustrations by Lesley Griffith
Photography by Andre Martin
Typeset in Australia by Asset Typesetting Pty Ltd
Printed in Australia by Impact Printing, Melbourne

National Library of Australia
Cataloguing-in-Publication data:

Cross, Diana.
Craft from recycled materials.

ISBN 1 86351 083 4.

1. Handicraft. 2. Recycling (Waste, etc.). I. Title.
(Series: Milner craft series).

745.58

ACKNOWLEDGEMENTS

This book is dedicated to my friends in the craft industry and is my way of saying thank you to: Anne Colligan, who designed and painted the assortment of recycled cans; Sandra Flannery and her daughter Debbie, who created the distinctive junk wall hangings and accept commissions (tel: (066) 76 6317); Lesley Griffith, the talented artist whose drawings grace the pages of this book; Amanda Ho, who supplied examples of découpage; Lyn Inall, a respected teacher of patchwork and quilting, who designed and made the bears and pillows from recycled denim and can be contacted on (062) 88 3497; Jean Kropper, who offers classes in papermaking and undertakes commissions for her original artwork (tel: (02) 427 7612); Denise Lawler, who designed and made the linen bear, silk tie photo album and picture frame and can be contacted at her shop 'Cottage Crafts' at Camden (tel: (046) 55 7071); Lorell McIntyre, who painted the spectacle lenses and the light globes; Lorraine Millar, who découpaged the glass plate; Glenda Overstead, who designed and made the beautiful christening set; Louise Owens; Irene Phipps; Pam Press; Susie Pullen, who supplied the silks and dyes for the button projects from Silk Road (tel: (043) 67 6449); Audrey Raymond, who supplied examples of découpage. The talents and materials these people so generously contributed have been greatly appreciated and admired.

The author and publisher are grateful to Caroline and Darryl Lobsey of Country Furniture Antiques, Balmain, for so generously allowing us to use their wonderful shop as the location for the photography; and to Michele Shennen's Garden Centres for supplying flowers for photography.

CONTENTS

———
———

INTRODUCTION

We have all heard our grandparents mention the good old days, when 'the only toys we had were the ones we made ourselves'. What wonderful toys they must have been, made with love and care, and treasured all the more because they were handmade. People used their imaginations and their hands to transform the old into the new.

We have a word for this nowadays: recycling. Recycling means using things again rather than throwing them away. As a result, fewer new raw materials are needed, less energy is used, and less pollution is caused. These facts should encourage most people to recycle, yet the number of products that end up as waste is increasing all the time. Many products are made to be used just once; many rapidly become outdated and must be replaced; others are wrapped in unnecessary packaging. Far too many end up as waste on our rubbish tips. Only a fraction of our waste is presently recycled.

Learn not to throw anything away before first considering its potential re-use. Organise the material — glass, paper, fabric, cans and so on — into separate storage containers. Recycling gives you the kind of satisfaction that goes with creating gifts, decorations, home decor items or new clothes, leaving a feeling of pride for having converted useless junk into something pretty and practical, or breathed new life into something that had seen better days. That is the real beauty of recycled craft: not only is it fun and relatively easy, but it costs almost nothing. The sky is the limit!

Whether you are looking for different types of crafts to try or simply for new ideas, this book will inspire you to create recycled craft items from everyday materials found around the home.

RECYCLED
paper

HANDMADE PAPER

The initial reaction of some people to the idea of handmaking paper may be 'why bother, when paper is so cheap and easy to purchase?' And of course the answer is that recycling paper saves one of the most precious elements of the environment. Every year, each one of us uses up to three trees for paper and cardboard. Waste paper tends to pile up at home and around the workplace, and most people have no idea of the practical ways in which this waste paper can be re-used, other than to leave it out for collection.

Making your own paper is inexpensive, creative and fun. Virtually any type of discarded paper can be turned into sheets of attractive writing paper, cards, labels and envelopes. Use waste material such as envelopes, manilla folders, photocopying paper, letters written on good quality writing paper, acid-free non-glossy junk mail. Once a mould and deckle has been made or purchased, the cost of the necessary materials is next to nothing.

Materials

• mould and deckle • blender or mixmaster • mixing bowl
• sieve • 2 buckets • waste paper to recycle • cup • colouring additive
such as tissues, food colouring, paper serviettes, coloured junk mail or
writing paper • tub, such as an old baby's bath, empty fish tank or
plastic box • waterproof apron and gloves • pressing boards — sheets
of marine timber larger than the mould • G-clamps or bricks
• pieces of linen or cotton cloth and old blanketing, both slightly larger
than the mould, OR blotting paper and sheets of newspaper
• small kitchen sponge • clothesline and pegs

General Instructions

Papermaking is messy, so set up outside in the laundry or garage. Wear a waterproof apron and shoes to prevent getting saturated, and gloves to protect your hands from chemicals that may be in the papers.

Prepare waste paper by taking gummed part and stamps off envelopes and checking for and removing the odd paper clip or staple. Tear all paper into small pieces, 2–3 cm (1–1½″) square, or collect shredded office paper. A little bit goes a long way, so to start with, one bucketful will be plenty. Put the paper in a bucket, add enough hot water to cover the paper, and leave to soak overnight until it is soft and mushy.

Take a small handful and place in the blender. Add fresh water to the correct level and blend in short bursts. If the blender seems to labour use less paper the next time, otherwise the motor will burn out. This blending breaks up the fibres in the paper and spreads them through the water. The smaller the paper pieces floating in the mixture the smoother the final paper will be. This blended mix is called pulp. Make sure the blender is cleaned thoroughly with disinfectant before being re-used in the kitchen, to remove any traces of chemicals from the paper.

Prepare the mould and deckle. The mould is a timber or stainless steel frame with a wire mesh stretched tightly over it to sieve the wet pulp. The deckle is another timber frame which fits onto the top of the mould. This gives the size limitations of the finished page, and also prevents the pulp from overflowing the mould.

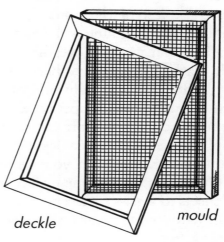

deckle   mould

Making paper pulp in blender

Mould and deckle

Tip the pulp into the tub. Continue to add pulp and enough water until the mixture is the consistency of thin porridge. If the mixture is too thick, add more water; if it's too thin, add more pulp.

Swish the pulp around in the tub then let it settle slightly. Holding the mould and deckle together tightly, lower it carefully down the side of the tub. Lift it slowly out of the water with the screen flat. Rest it on the edge of the tub and wait for most of the water to drain through. The screen should be covered with an even sheet of pulp. If it isn't, tip it back and start again.

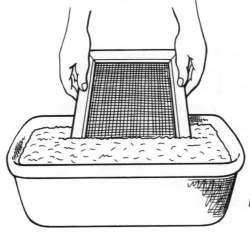

Lowering mould and deckle into tub

Prepare the pressing boards by covering one board with two wet pieces of blanketing and one wet piece of cloth, or put some blotting paper on top of several layers of newspaper. Lift the deckle off the mould, leaving the sheet of recycled paper on the mesh. Turn the mould quickly upside down and tip the paper onto the cloth. Gently sponge the mesh and squeeze out the excess water. Carefully lift off the mould by first pressing then rocking the mould back and forth.

Cover the sheet of paper with another cloth. Repeat from the beginning as often as you like, finishing with a piece of cloth on top, more blanketing, and finally the other pressing board. Clamp together or place bricks on top to remove the last of the water. Leave for several hours tilted at an angle. The amount of drying time will depend on the weather. When the paper feels damp rather than wet, remove the boards and hang up the individual pieces of cloth, each holding one sheet of paper, on a clothesline. Leave until thoroughly dry, then carefully peel off the paper and flatten between books. Alternatively, use blotting paper on either side of the mushy paper and a rolling pin to squeeze out some more of the water. Turn the blotting paper over and iron until the recycled paper between it is nearly dry. Peel off the top piece of blotting paper and leave your recycled paper in a warm place to finish drying. If you wish to have one surface of the paper smooth for writing, transfer the wet sheets to a glass surface to dry.

Plain leftover pulp can be drained, sealed in a plastic bag and stored in the fridge or freezer for another time.

Decorated paper

- Add fresh or dried herbs, spices, flowers or tea leaves to the pulp mixture before blending. These will give a flecked, often scented result to the sheet of recycled paper. Adding perfume oil to the tub of pulp gives a scented result, too.
- For heavyweight paper, recycle cardboard and cartons.
- Mix different types of waste paper together to give a mottled effect.
- Add glitter to the tub to give the paper a sparkle.
- Collect waste paper of particular colours; use it to make recycled paper of the same colour, or combine for a multicoloured effect.
- Wonderful raised or depressed impressions can be formed on the paper by placing objects such as leaves, lace doilies, lengths of lace or string on top of the wet paper, then covering with a cloth and pressing board. Also, laying wet paper on a moistened textured cloth such as hessian or netting will result in an interesting all-over surface effect.
- Make double sided paper by placing one thin sheet of wet paper on top of another. These may even be of two different colours.
- Make one thin sheet of wet paper and place items such as leaves, feathers, ribbons or old used Christmas cards on top. Lay another sheet of paper on top. While the paper is still wet, use your fingers to carefully peel off small sections of the top layer to reveal pieces of the underlying item, such as the central picture of a card.

- Change the size and shape of the final recycled sheet of paper by making a 'stencil' from sticky Contact paper. Cut a piece the size of the mould. Cut out a new shape such as an oval or an opened-out envelope. Stick it onto the screen, then proceed as normal. When the mould and deckle is lifted up through the tub the pulp will slide off the slippery Contact-covered areas, leaving the cut-out shape.
- To make paper easier to write on, add sizing to the pulp. A simple size can be made by mixing 1½ to 2 heaped tablespoons of cornflour or instant starch powder to cold water. Boil until the mixture has a fairly thin consistency and looks translucent. Add this mix to the pulp in the tub. Sizing is a water-resistant substance which prevents ink from spreading over the surface of the paper.

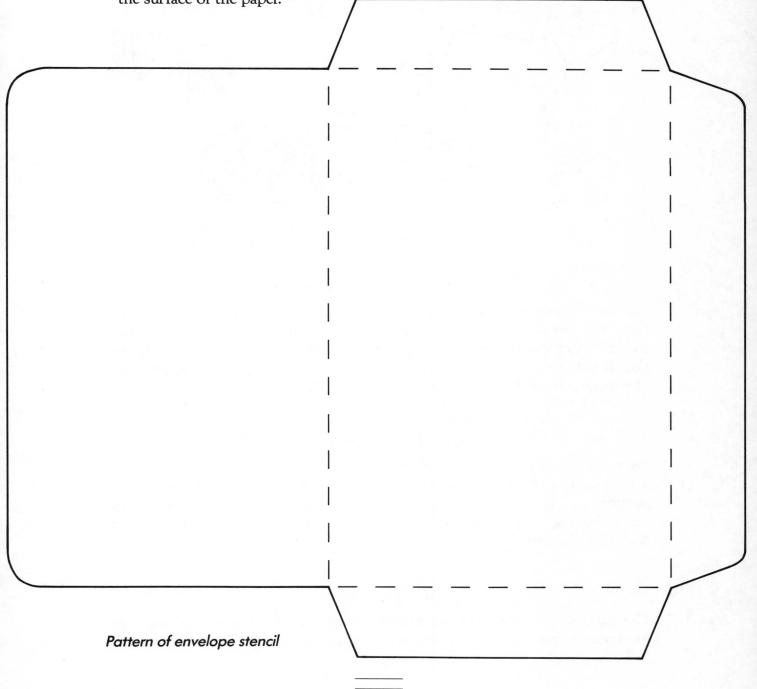

Pattern of envelope stencil

Fun ideas to do with handmade paper

Cookie-cutter shapes

Place cookie-cutter shapes on top of the mould screen. Pour the pulp mixture from the tub into the shape until the required thickness is reached. Leave to drain. Remove the shape and turn the mould upside down on the drying boards as before. When they are dry, use these shapes to decorate other sheets of paper, or hang them as decorations or a mobile, or frame them as a picture.

Personalised stationery

Personalise sheets of recycled paper by embossing initials in one corner. Use a purchased alphabet stencil and an embossing tool or the blunt end of a paintbrush. Place the stencil in position on the wrong side of the paper. With the embossing tool, gently push the paper out to the right side within each section of the stencil.

Gift bag

The simplicity of this gift bag shows the texture of the recycled paper to maximum effect. From the pantry cupboard, choose a box with dimensions to fit the gift. Wrap the paper around the box, allowing an overlap at the back, and glue in place where the paper overlaps. The paper should extend about 2.5 cm (1″) beyond the end of the box. To make the base of the bag, fold in the paper at the sides, bring up the bottom flap and glue down the top flap. Slip the box out. Crease in the sides of the bag so that it partially collapses. Enclose the gift. Fold over a flap at the top of the bag and punch a hole in the middle of the folded area. Close the bag with a coloured cord. For that added effect, glue on a tiny fan made out of recycled paper. To make the fan, tear a small rectangle of recycled paper and crease into narrow concertina folds. Pinch one end together and glue. Spread out the other end. (As you can see from the colour photographs, these fans look most effective when the pinched end is coloured.)

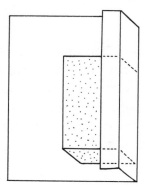

wrap paper around a box

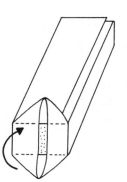

fold in paper at the ends

glue down top and bottom flaps

crease in sides of bag

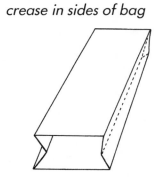

Bag formation

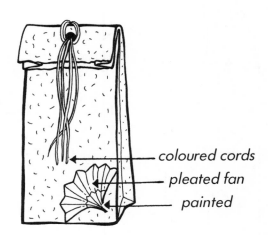

coloured cords
pleated fan
painted

Paper collage

Collect an assortment of handmade papers and transform them into a collage of colour and texture by arranging them into geometric or abstract shapes. Small parcels can be formed by tearing strips of three different widths from papers of three different colours. Layer them by placing the widest on the bottom and the narrowest on the top, then roll them up. Glue at the back, wrap a length of cording around, and tie a simple knot. Cut a strip of cardboard and cover it with the same three coloured papers. Wrap the cording along the length as shown. As a final embellishment, add a large knot with exaggerated loops and long tails. The collage can appear stark or subdued, depending on the placement of the components and the use of warm or cool colours. Ideas for the collage will flow as you move the pieces around on a background. Do not rush the final arrangement. When you are satisfied, carefully glue each piece into place on another sheet of handmade paper, such as the oval shape in the photograph. Leave a border around the collage so that the framing does not detract from the three-dimensional effect.

Gift box

Transfer the pattern for the box onto a sheet of fairly thick handmade paper. Score or mark the fold lines on the wrong side of the paper. Turn the paper over to the right side and glue tab A where indicated to form the main part of the box. Fold flaps B and C inward. Finish off the base by inserting tab D into box. Repeat this for the top of the box, after enclosing the gift. Decorate the box with a fan (see instructions under *Gift bag*) or curled ribbons.

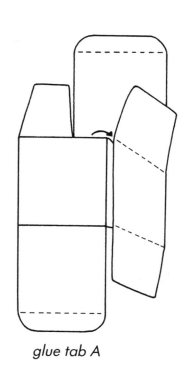

glue tab A

Gift box formation

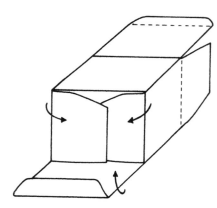

fold flap B and C inwards.
Insert tab D

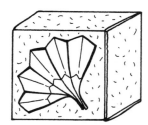

finished box decorated with
a paper fan

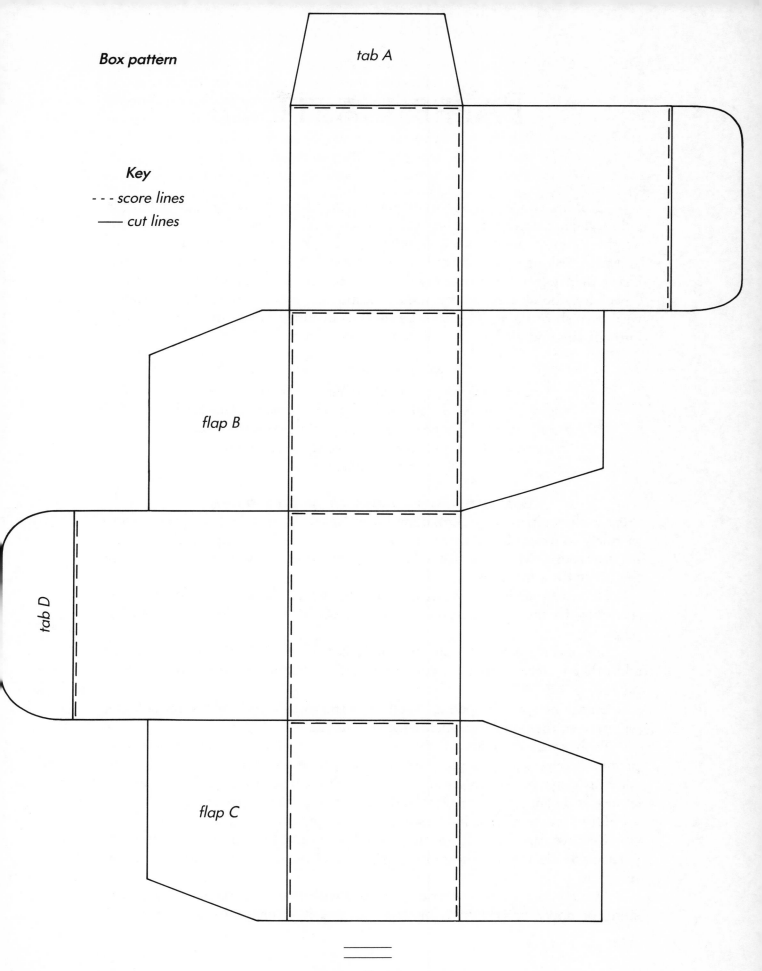

Box pattern

tab A

Key
- - - score lines
——— cut lines

flap B

tab D

flap C

PAPER CASTING

*T*his is a form of three-dimensional paper art using recycled paper pulp, which dries hard. It has the detailed look of cast plaster without the weight. A mixture of pulp and sizing, rather like clay, is pressed into small individual baking or shortbread moulds available from kitchen specialty shops. Using pulp paper for moulds with fine detail gives a very satisfactory result. Once dry, the shapes can be removed and left natural or made waterproof with varnish or paint. They can be used to decorate boxes and parcels, made into gift tags and mobiles, or painted and then framed.

Materials
• *recycled paper pulp* • *small biscuit or shortbread moulds*
• *spray can of cooking oil* • *small kitchen sponge* • *mixing bowl*
• *wallpaper paste in powder form (sizing)* • *sieve* • *water-based*
varnish or PVA glue (optional) • *acrylic paints (optional)*
• *gesso (optional)*

General Instructions
Prepare the pulp as in papermaking (see pages 2-3), blending the paper pieces as finely as possible so there are no lumps. Strain the pulp until no water seeps through. Make enough pulp for a few projects, as it can be stored in the fridge for a few days.

Place the pulp in a bowl and mix in sizing (which should have been prepared according to the manufacturer's instructions). This will add strength to the pulp.

Stir and squeeze the pulp until it feels malleable. At this stage, you can add other materials to the pulp to give colour, texture or scent, as described on page 4.

Smear or spray a coating of oil over the inside areas of the mould; this will prevent the pulp from sticking to the mould.

Push small amounts of the pulp well into all the mould impressions, pressing down with a slightly moistened sponge to remove as much excess water as possible. Try to create an even, well-compacted layer. Wring out the sponge and continue absorbing the water until the pulp is just damp.

Dry for several days in the sun or in a warm, well-ventilated room.

Remove the pulp from the mould and dry further. If the mould is particularly deep, ease the pulp gently away from the sides with a knife to release it.

If the paper shape is to be decorated with paint, brush or spray it with sizing or apply several coats of gesso to give it a non-absorbent surface. A thin shape can be made more rigid by coating each side with sizing. Once the shape is painted, allow the surface to dry then seal it with a water-based varnish or some PVA glue mixed with water.

Decorations

Punch or pierce two adjacent holes towards the top of the shape for threading ribbons to hang. If the decoration is left in its natural state it may be necessary to seal the edges of the holes with glue or sizing to prevent tearing.

Greeting cards

Fold a sheet of recycled paper in half and seal with sizing. Glue a shape to the front and add an appropriate message.

Decorated book or folder

Glue a shape on the cover of a book or folder to make an interesting gift or to brighten up your own journal, note book or recipe collection etc.

Gift cards

Back the shapes with a slightly larger piece of coloured cardboard. Punch a hole in one end of the cardboard, thread through a cord and write the message on the back.

Fun things to do with paper casting

PAPER PULP MODELLING

*O*nce some of the excess water is removed from the paper pulp and sizing added, the pulp can be manipulated much like clay. Free-form objects can be created by simply squeezing and shaping the pulp, but to create large objects you must support the damp pulp. Once dry and hardened, the objects can be sanded gently then painted and sealed.

Materials
• *recycled paper pulp* • *sieve* • *wallpaper paste (sizing)* • *mixing bowl*
• *spray can of cooking oil* • *small kitchen sponge* • *aluminium foil*

General Instructions
Cover the workbench with greased aluminium foil. This will help you to release the object after it has dried.

Prepare the pulp as for paper casting (see pages 2-3).

Squeeze and shape the pulp to create the object. Leave to dry.

Jewellery

Using paper pulp as a base for jewellery gives a degree of freedom in the shape and size of the pieces, as they are so light to wear. When dry they can be sealed, painted and varnished. Pierce a hole to thread a chain, or glue on the appropriate brooch or earring findings, before decorating the individual pieces. Sequins, metallic threads, buttons, charms, beads or stones can be embedded in the piece while it is damp or glued on after it is dry.

Decorations

Brush a water-based glue over the surface of a foam shape. Apply a thin, even coat of paper pulp so that it completely covers the shape. Press the surface with a sponge to remove excess water and to give better adhesion to the foam. Attach a paper clip to the top as a hanger. For a Santa head (see drawing), add more texture by forming the beard and moustache with paper pulp. When dry, seal, paint and varnish. Then add extra features such as Santa's hat and bell.

felt hat

pompom

white fur fabric

painted facial features

paper pulp beard

Santa decoration

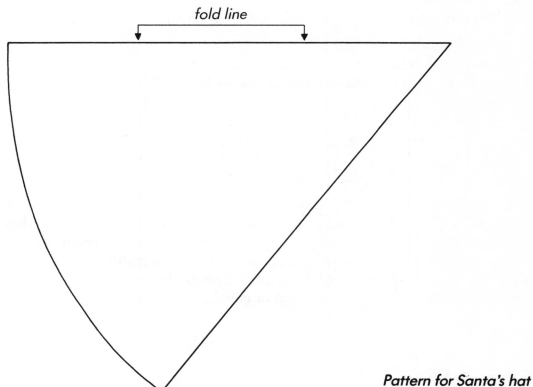

fold line

Pattern for Santa's hat

Beads

Model a variety of bead shapes in paper pulp. Allow to dry and harden. Rub with fine sandpaper if a smooth finish is desired. Before painting, make a hole in each bead with a compass point or a strong needle so that they are ready to thread.

GIFT BAG PICTURES

*T*he most wonderful assortment of gift bags made of high-gloss paper, featuring beautiful designs, is available in card and gift shops. As these are fairly expensive, it seems a shame — and a waste — just to throw them out after the gift has been received. Why not make an eye-catching collage out of a single bag or a group.

Instructions

Mount the bag on a piece of coloured matt board which blends in with or highlights the design on the bag. Glue the handles in position.

Add a bow to complement the colours of the bag and pop a crushed paper flower inside the bag. Glue in place.

Have the completed collage professionally framed.

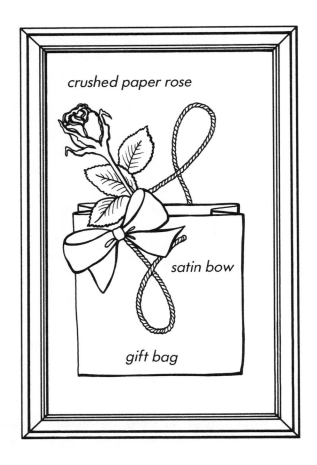

Paper gift bag

PAPER BEADS

*I*n every home at the end of each year there is a pile of outdated magazines under the coffee table. By all means tear out articles that may be useful for future reference, but before throwing the rest of the magazines away or donating them to the local dentist's waiting room, try the old craft of making paper beads. This requires very little in the way of raw materials and gives a lot of fun. It involves coiling a long tapering triangle of paper around a temporary core made of a cylindrical rod or wire. The bead changes shape as the paper coil builds up.

Materials
• *pages from old magazines* • *white glue (PVA)* • *brush* • *scissors*
• *thick wire* • *elastic bands* • *cardboard* • *clear varnish*

Instructions

Make a cardboard template of each of the long triangles (see patterns). With these as a guide, cut a number of triangles from a variety of pages in the magazine. Each triangle forms one bead, and each bead will be different, depending on the page chosen. Interesting effects are created when just black and white printing is used, or a particularly predominant colour, or a combination of both.

Take one triangle, wrong side up, and fold the base end around the wire or rod. Begin gently, to make sure the bead builds up evenly. Continue to roll the paper tightly until the last 8–10 cm (4"). Brush the wrong side of this remaining length of paper with glue and roll to the end.

Remove the finished bead from the wire or rod and leave to dry. When the beads are dry, they will be hard enough to sandpaper smooth.

Give the beads 1–3 coats of varnish to protect and harden them. Leave to dry threaded on the wire or rod, separated by wound elastic bands.

The beads can then be strung as necklaces, bracelets or earrings. You can also alternate the paper beads with commercial ones.

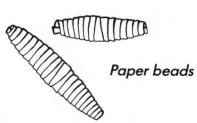

Paper beads

Patterns for paper beads

RECYCLED CARDS

*A*t any celebration, greeting cards are opened with great enthusiasm, displayed prominently for all to admire — and then, alas, discarded as rubbish. Often, these cards are gifts expressing a special thought, or they are very beautiful in themselves. Store treasured cards; with a little imagination and patience, they can be transformed into many things. They can be reused as greeting cards, framed as a collage, cut out for table decorations, made into a toy, or used in découpage. A fun way to begin is to group these cards by theme, colour or design.

Table place cards

These add that touch of charm and colour to a special occasion, such as a Christmas dinner or a child's birthday party. Keep all cards with suitable themes. Trim each card to a size relative in width and twice the height of a place card. With small embroidery scissors, cut only the details around the top half of the central design or character on the card. Try to remove as much of the background as you can. Fold this top half of the background down to form a stand-up place card. Leave enough room at the base to write the guest's name.

If cutting away the background is not possible, cut out the character completely and glue it onto a folded piece of cardboard. Leave space at the side for the guest's name.

Either card can be accented with paint, lace, ribbons, glitter, or anything else that you can think of.

Table place cards

cut around details from top half of card

fold top half of background down

cut out character completely and glue onto a plain card

Fun things to make with recycled cards

Bookmark

With small embroidery scissors, carefully cut out an attractive scene or a lovable character. Glue this to a strip of ribbon in a complementary colour.

Flower picks

Varnish card cutouts and mount them on blunt ends of timber skewers. Use the pointed ends to stick into a flower arrangement. Choose cutouts appropriate to the occasion.

Greeting card gallery

Among your saved cards will be those unmarked by messages, making them suitable for framing individually or as a collection. Back the card with mounting board at least 2–3 cm (at least 1″) wider all around than the card, then frame. Another idea is to glue a relatively plain wrapping paper to cardboard as a mounting board and place in a purchased clip frame. If a more Victorian effect is desired, the card can be mounted on a lace doily or a piece of velvet before framing with extras such as ribbons, flowers, charms and beads glued on.

Puzzle blocks

To make a set of puzzle blocks, you need four wooden cubes and six greeting cards. Each card is divided into quarters so that each card quarter is the same size as each cube face. Glue the four quarters of each card to faces on different cubes. Smooth out all the air bubbles and wrinkles with your fingers. Let the blocks dry. Finish with two or three coats of varnish, following the manufacturer's instructions. The puzzle is to arrange the cubes to recreate the original card picture.

New cards from old

Cut out a section of an old card and glue or stitch it to a folded sheet of recycled paper or cardboard to create a totally new card.

DÉCOUPAGE

Découpage, the turn of the century pastime of decorating with paper cutouts, is experiencing renewed popularity at present. This craft epitomises the concept of recycling: you take used pictures, papers and prints from various sources and glue them to an assortment of ordinary old items, and the result is wonderful new treasures with an antique, elegant, old world look.

Traditional découpage came to prominence in Europe in the seventeenth and eighteenth centuries. Sections from exquisite papers, cards and prints were cut out in very fine detail, carefully arranged and glued onto pieces of furniture, then covered with many coats of varnish to give the impression of expensive handpainted Oriental lacquerwork. These successive coats of varnish are built up over the cutouts, disguising the thickness of the papers, until the cutouts appear to recede and become part of the background. The resulting surface will feel mirror smooth and will be extremely durable after curing.

Découpage has many advantages as a craft: it is relatively simple and inexpensive in terms of raw materials and equipment, and with little artistic ability you can create beautiful objects that have a handpainted look. As each decorated piece needs up to fifty coats of varnish, however, a certain amount of time and patience is required, and some of the more ornate pieces, involving

RECYCLED CARDS: *(back wall)* MOUNTED AND FRAMED CARD; *(top shelf)* FLOWER PICKS; *(bench)* TABLE PLACE CARD AND PUZZLE BLOCKS; AND *(on bear)* PAPER BEADS FROM RECYCLED MAGAZINES

DECOUPAGED OBJECTS: (*background*) SERVING TRAY;
(*top shelf*) JAPANESE-STYLE CONTAINER WITH LID, SMALL DOOR
KNOBS, SMALL CASE AND TERRACOTTA POT; (*bottom*) CHEST AND
BRIEFCASE, DOOR KNOBS, JEWELLERY BOX, HAIR SLIDE, BROOCHES,
EGG, TRINKET BOXES, DOOR FINGER PLATES AND
RIVER STONE PAPERWEIGHTS

ASSORTED RECYCLED PAPER: PAPER CAST TEDDY BEARS, HEARTS
AND BUTTERFLY, HANDMADE PAPER - ROLLED AND SHEETS,
MOULDED PAPER JEWELLERY, PAPER DECORATED WITH FEATHERS
AND PAPER DECORATED WITH DOILY IMPRESSIONS

many layers of cutouts, do need an understanding of colour and design. But few crafts are as satisfying or give such an urge to lovingly touch the finished piece.

Possible sources of good quality paper cutouts are endless. Save and recycle gift wrapping papers, greeting cards, special invitations, shop and mail order catalogues, colourful travel brochures, postcards, photographs, outdated calendars, old stamps and labels, illustrations from damaged or cheap books, quality magazine pictures, old letters and even cherished sheet music. Almost any smooth, hard surface can be a background for découpage, including timber, glass, bisque or glazed porcelain, firm leather, simple shells, primed metal, flat plastic, smooth river rocks, plaster masks, mirrors and papier mâché. It's a challenge to track down suitable objects from around the home, in secondhand shops, on holidays and other outings, and at auctions.

Materials

• *item to be decorated* • *good quality pictures*
• *sandpaper (wet and dry): No. 400, No. 600, No. 1200*
• *No. 000 steel wool* • *acrylic sealer* • *small sharp scissors with straight blade* • *sharp cuticle scissors with curved blade* • *tweezers*
• *roller* • *Blu-tack* • *Aquadhere glue (PVA) or wallpaper paste*
• *a good, appropriately sized brush for applying glue, sealer and varnish* • *sponge* • *matt or semi gloss varnish (turps based)*
• *acrylic or oil paints* • *turps for cleaning* • *razor blade* • *tack cloth*
• *toothpick or cotton bud* • *coloured pencils or paints to conceal white paper edges* • *for timber items: wood putty, furniture wax, antique glaze*

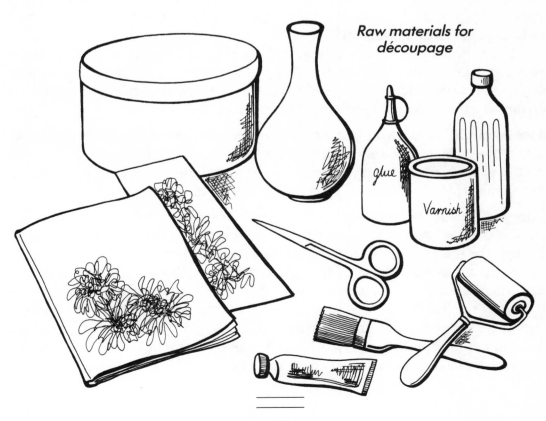

Raw materials for découpage

General Instructions

Selecting a project: From the list given in the introduction, choose an object that is suited to your level of expertise. If you are a beginner, select something that has one flat surface to découpage.

Preparing a timber surface: If the object you have chosen is made of timber, check it over and remove any hinges, handles or other hardware if possible. The surface must be sanded smooth, with all holes and scratches filled with wood putty. A very bad surface can be given a coat of gesso.

If the timber is to be stained, do not use a sealer. If the timber is to be left in its natural state, lightly sand it with a fine sandpaper. Work back and forth along the grain. Remove the dust then apply two coats of sealer, each in opposite directions. Alternatively you can paint the background with an acrylic paint. Seal the timber first, then paint using a colour that will enhance the cutouts. When it is thoroughly dry, sand again, wipe clean and apply a second coat of paint. Finish with a coat of sealer. If required, paint or line the inside of the object. Remount the hardware.

Selecting and preparing the paper cutouts: Spend time in the selection, and start with designs with clear outlines which will be easy to cut. Group the cutouts according to a theme, such as flowers and fruits, Australiana, Victoriana, Oriental designs, borders and abstract patterns. Keep the cutouts stored flat in individual subject folders — this will save you time in the future. Choose a design that suits the object to be decorated. Be as creative as you can when you plan the finished découpage picture. Use one design or several, overlapping if desired.

All cutouts should be on fairly thin paper, to decrease the number of coats of varnish needed to cover the paper thickness. Thick postcards, greeting cards and photographs must be soaked in water for some time to enable the backing paper to be peeled off.

The thin papers of magazines must be sealed and the backs painted white to prevent any print bleeding through after varnishing. Using a brush, seal all papers on both sides to prevent damage to the design during gluing. Sealing strengthens the paper and prevents discoloration.

Backgrounds: Before you begin to découpage, you can finish the background of the object in any of several ways. Use plain paint, pearlised paint, pretend crackling, gold or silver leaf, or marbling. Any of these treatments will enhance the overall effect.

Cutting: This is the most important part of découpage. Relax, take your time and use good scissors. Cutting must be a continuous action, moving the paper through the scissors rather than the scissors around the paper.

With straight-bladed scissors, cut away the excess paper around the design area, then use curved scissors — with the curved point facing outwards — to cut out the interior design detail. Work from the centre out. Leave 'bridges' of paper to support the finer sections of the design; when you are ready to glue the cutout you can cut away these bridges. Always allow yourself plenty of choice by having more cutouts than you need.

Conceal the white cut edges of the paper cutouts with an appropriately coloured pencil or paint. If you do not do this the white edges will show through after varnishing.

Picture layout: Using tweezers, arrange the cutouts into a picture on the object. Move them about until the picture is pleasing, beginning with the larger elements and ending with the smaller ones and the fine trims. Hold all the pieces in place with Blu-tack.

Gluing: On the surface of the object, carefully outline each cutout with chalk as a guideline for gluing. Always put a thin coat of glue on the surface to be découpaged, not on the paper cutouts. Glue one cutout at a time.

With the tweezers, place the cutouts in position. Put a dob of glue on the top of the cutout then rub with your finger tips to spread it evenly. Start from the centre of the cutout and smooth towards the edges, carefully removing any air bubbles.

After the cutouts have set for a few minutes, pat them gently with a damp sponge to remove all excess glue from the surface. Check that all edges are glued down by touching up with a little bit of glue on the end of a toothpick. Leave to dry thoroughly. Seal the entire object again for added protection before varnishing.

Fun things to découpage

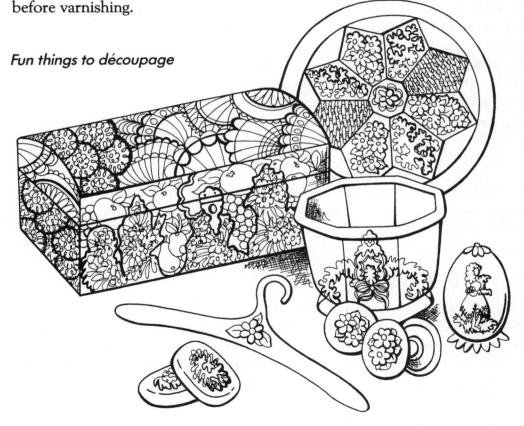

Varnishing and sanding: The aim of découpage is to achieve a silky, high gloss surface similar to French polishing or the lacquered Oriental finish. Begin by applying several coats of varnish. Use a paint brush and dip the brush only halfway into the varnish, pressing it against the sides of the can to remove any excess.

Apply a thin film of varnish with long flowing strokes. All the strokes should be in one direction; you change direction with each successive coat of varnish. Be very careful not to form air bubbles, as once these have dried on the surface they are permanent.

Squeeze the brush out and suspend it in turps before re-using. Allow each coat of varnish to dry for at least 24 hours before starting the next. The surface must be dusted with a cloth between each coat of varnish.

Repeat these steps for about ten coats of varnish, until the design has sunk beneath the surface of the varnish. You can now begin sandpapering. This is to get an even, level coat by removing dust and imperfections such as small bubbles. Begin by sanding lightly with No. 400 wet/dry sandpaper dampened with water. Add a bit of detergent to help eliminate tiny scratch marks. Sand only along the grain if you are découpaging timber. Clean the surface with a damp sponge and leave to dry.

Continue to varnish, sanding in this way after every third coat until a total of 16 coats have been applied. Apply 6 more coats before sanding again.

After 22 coats, the surface should be smooth. If it is not, continue varnishing until the paper can no longer be felt. Change to No. 600 wet/dry sandpaper and apply 7 more coats of varnish, sanding between each one.

Now change to No. 1200 wet/dry sandpaper and apply another 3 coats, sanding between each one. After varnishing, clean the brush well in mineral turpentine.

For the final sanding, use No. 000 steel wool to remove all traces of gloss. When the surface is silky smooth and uniformly dull, wipe clean with a soft cloth and allow to dry.

Waxing: The object can now be polished with a high-quality wax or furniture polish for a final high gloss finish. Do not put anything on top of the object for at least six months — it takes this long to cure.

Final touches: To further decorate and add to the individual character of the object, some beautiful hardware such as metal appliques, hinges and handles is available on the market.

Patchwork timber serving tray

Carefully draw one of the simpler patchwork designs onto a sheet of cardboard. Cut out the individual design components and use these pieces of card as templates. Trace each component onto the back of a coordinated selection of used papers of similar thickness. Cut out these paper patches and assemble them on the tray, reproducing the original patchwork design.

Timber jewellery

Mount any paper cutouts onto pieces of timber jewellery. The design must be appropriate to the size and shape of the jewellery. Often, patterned papers just cut into geometric shapes create a striking effect.

Plasticware

Clean the surface thoroughly with warm water and a mild soap. Wipe dry. Glue prints to plastic with an acrylic polymer emulsion. Apply fewer coats of varnish than for timber and do not wax.

Decorated soap

Apply two coats of water-based varnish. Glue the cutouts onto the soap with Aquadhere. Varnish with 4 to 6 coats only. The découpage will last the life of the soap.

Porcelain (bisque or glazed)

Seal the porcelain with acrylic spray or a special ceramic sealer only if unglazed. Before and after filling any holes, sand the surface smooth with No. 400 wet/dry sandpaper. If desired, paint the background with acrylic paint before starting the découpage.

Door knobs

Ceramic door handles and previously varnished or untreated timber can be découpaged.

Eggs

Prepare hen or goose eggs by making a hole in the top and bottom with a skewer. Blow through one hole, forcing out the contents through the other one. Clean the insides thoroughly. Clean the outside with a cream cleanser. Paint the shell with at least three thin coats of acrylic paint, drying between each one. Seal the shell before starting the découpage.

Papier mâché

Seal all papier mâché items well before beginning to découpage. Do not attempt to sand the item until the cutouts are completely covered, as the surface of papier mâché is very delicate.

Terracotta pots

As terracotta is porous and particularly vulnerable to seepage, the pot must be painted inside and out with several coats of sealer.

RECYCLED *fabric*

RECYCLED LINEN AND TIES

*A*rdent quilters, sewers and general hoarders will tuck away any interesting or antique pieces of fabric, many with a sentimental story to tell. Even undamaged scraps of old, stained and worn-out but treasured quilts can be recycled. Often, old clothes are thrown away simply because they are out of fashion or too small, not because they are worn out. Some of these can be painstakingly pulled apart and made into new clothes. You may have pillow case sets or fine handkerchiefs, delicately embroidered and edged, which have been lovingly stored away in drawers because they are too pretty to throw away but too out of date or impractical to use. If you're lucky, auctions can also be the source of bundles of doilies and hankies at very reasonable prices.

In this chapter, fabrics such as ties, bed and table linens, laces, hankies and old clothing are innovatively recycled. Ties are unpicked, cut and restitched; linens are cleaned, spots and rust marks cut away and the rest utilised; doilies and exquisite lengths of lace restitched; hankies and old pillow cases cleverly transformed into cherished dolls. Completed items using recycled fabric often hold pleasurable family memories.

Another excellent way to recycle many of these fabrics is by using the crazy patchwork technique of the Victorian era. This form of patchwork incorporates different types and irregularly shaped pieces of fabric in a totally random fashion. The predominant feature of any crazy patchwork is the opulence of embellishment, including a variety of embroidery stitches covering every seam as well as scattered over the surface. Sequins, pearls, beads, laces, ribbons, buttons, charms and other doodads are added in layers, giving a wonderful feeling of texture, colour and interest.

A frequent problem with old fabrics is the discoloration that comes with age. There are a number of ways to clean these stains from light-coloured fabrics, but if all fail you can always camouflage the mark by dyeing the whole piece in tea, which will give it a lovely, soft, mellow look. Add instant tea bags to boiling water, double the strength recommended for making tea. Dip the fabric into the warm tea, stir and leave to soak for 15 to 30 minutes, checking every 5 minutes or so for depth of colour. When the fabric has absorbed enough colour, squeeze out the excess tea, rinse thoroughly and wrap in a dry towel to absorb more moisture and tea residue. Dry in a dryer or with an iron.

'Having always loved old doilies and linens, it always seemed a shame that with deterioration over the years all the beautiful handiwork of ladies in times past was left unused and unwanted in a cupboard. Crazy patchwork became a passion for me some years ago, and in

the quest for embellishments for projects I found table centres, handkerchiefs, doilies and other linen a marvellous source by selecting the best parts and discarding the rest. Of course, undamaged heirloom pieces remained untouched. But I gladly sorted through secondhand stores and antique shops for pieces with rust or holes which could be cut away, leaving plenty of usable fabric.'

Denise Lawler

'There are many reasons for using recycled clothing: hard economic times, the challenge of creating something new from old, and preserving old fabrics and laces. Historically, through the hard times, we read of clothing being cut down and remade so it is not a new idea, but it certainly is a practical one. The materials for the christening set (see page 34) were collected from several sources, among them opportunity shops and friends' rag bags. Friends dug deep into their rag bags for old dresses. It was fascinating to see and feel these dresses, some of them probably dating back to the 1930s. While I was stitching my thoughts often wandered, speculating where and when the garments had been used and by whom. The challenge was to make the best use of each piece of fabric and at the same time preserve its own character.'

Glenda Overstead

Linen bear

Based on a commercial pattern, but using doilies, crocheted centrepieces, embroidered tablemats and cloths as embellishments, this delightful handmade bear is reminiscent of the Victorian era, when crazy patchwork quilts graced many homes.

Materials
• commercial bear pattern • old doilies, crocheted centrepieces, embroidered tablemats and cloths • stuffing • plain calico as a base • satin ribbon for a bow • small charm

Instructions
Take any commercial bear pattern that appeals to you and cut the body pieces out in calico. Decide which of the pieces of linen and crochet are the prettiest, or have the most embroidery on them. Place these in prominent positions where they will be appreciated best, such as face, chest, feet pads and inner arms. Cover each pattern piece with the different selected fabrics, having cut them into a variety of sizes and shapes. Make sure that each one overlays the previous one and that all raw cut edges are concealed by the decorative finished edges of other pieces. See the diagram of the bear front and back as a guide for placement.

With matching cotton, hand or machine sew the patchwork pieces

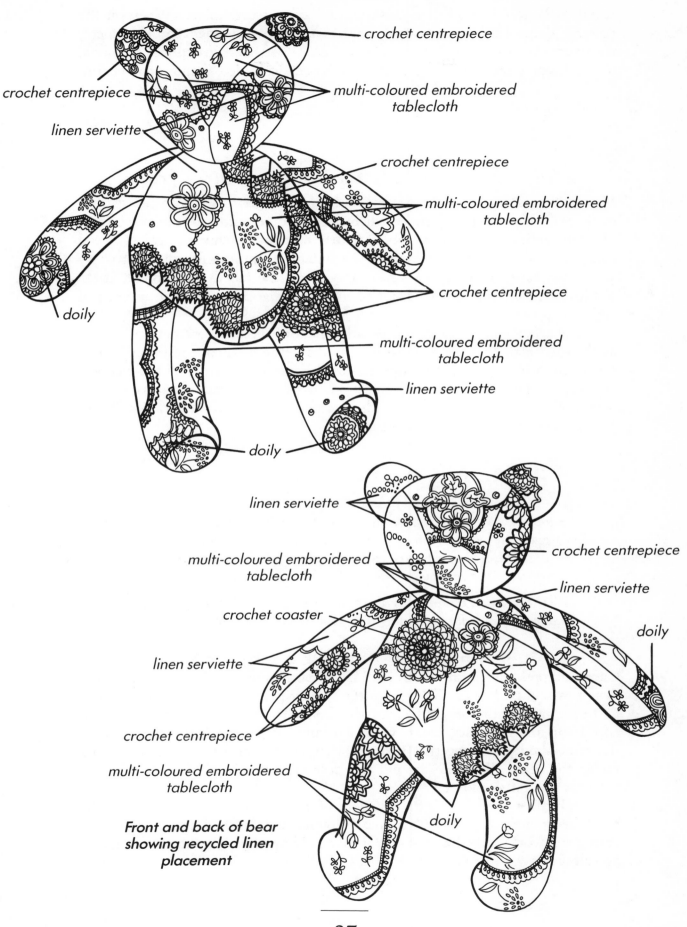

crochet centrepiece

crochet centrepiece

multi-coloured embroidered tablecloth

linen serviette

crochet centrepiece

multi-coloured embroidered tablecloth

crochet centrepiece

doily

multi-coloured embroidered tablecloth

linen serviette

doily

linen serviette

crochet centrepiece

multi-coloured embroidered tablecloth

linen serviette

crochet coaster

doily

linen serviette

crochet centrepiece

multi-coloured embroidered tablecloth

doily

Front and back of bear showing recycled linen placement

together. Follow a stitch line close to the edge of each piece. When all the pattern pieces have been covered with some form of linen embellishment, construct the bear according to the commercial pattern instructions. As a final touch, fasten a satin bow around the bear's neck, complete with a small charm.

Silk tie photo album and picture frame

Men's silk ties change with fashions and generally get tossed into the rag bag or sent off to opportunity shops when they become outdated. But ties consist of a fair amount of fabric, suitable for making crazy patchwork projects. And every part of a tie can be recycled. The linings are wonderful for embroidery and often have brand names superimposed on the fabric. Save these labels; stitched in rows separated by strips of contrasting fabric, they make an unusual embellishment for a jacket.

The actual shape of a tie suggests the traditional patchwork pattern known as Dresden Plate. So this pattern was used for the front of the photo album cover and around the picture opening of the frame, showing off the richness of the ties' fabrics. Sew on a collection of odds and ends such as ribbon, lace, doilies, charms, buttons, braids and beads, plus ribbon and silk thread embroidery, to create original craft items.

Materials

Picture frame: • old picture frame • old silk ties (unpicked) • brocade fabric to complement the ties • wadding • glue • cardboard • gathered lace, 2.5 cm (1") wide • embellishments such as charms, seed beads, tiny pearls, buttons • silk ribbon for embroidery • embroidery threads • embroidery needle

Photo album cover: • as above, replacing picture frame with photo album • cords for decorating the spine • tassel • narrow gold braid

General Instructions

Clean and press all the unpicked ties. Make a cardboard template of the Dresden Plate petals in both sizes. (The size of the smaller petals will have to be adjusted to fit an oval photo insert.) From the ties, cut 21 petals in the small size and 16 in the large size, both with a 6 mm (¼") seam allowance. Join all the same-sized petals together to form a circle or oval. Press all seams. Turn under the seam allowance around the pointed outer edge of the circle and stitch on the gathered lace.

Embroider the seams with a variety of stitches and add other embellishments as indicated on the diagrams. Appliqué the finished circle or oval of crazy patchwork onto the brocade fabric, ready for covering the picture frame and album.

28

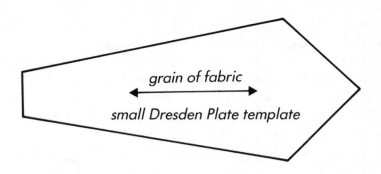

grain of fabric

small Dresden Plate template

*add 6 mm (¼") seam
allowances*

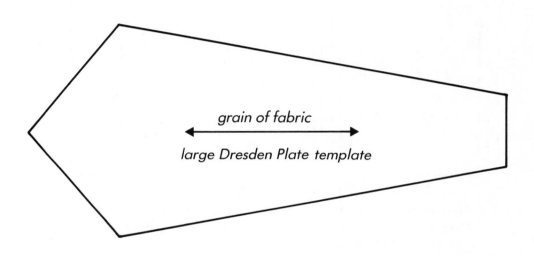

grain of fabric

large Dresden Plate template

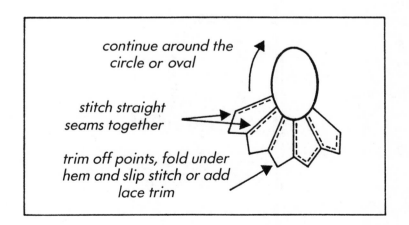

*continue around the
circle or oval*

*stitch straight
seams together*

*trim off points, fold under
hem and slip stitch or add
lace trim*

**Oval assembly of Dresden
Plate petals**

Instructions

Picture frame cover: Cut heavy cardboard to fit inside the frame as a mattboard. Cut an oval shape in the centre for the picture. Cut wadding the same shape as the cardboard and glue it in place. Cut fabric 2 or 3 cm (about 1″) larger than the wadded cardboard, around the outer edge as well as the oval centre. Make small cuts around the oval and glue the inner edges of the fabric to the back of the mattboard. Mitre the corners and glue the outer edges of the fabric to the back of the mattboard. Pull the fabric firmly so that the frame is covered neatly, without any creases.

Whether or not you can put glass over this will depend on the depth of the frame and the thickness of the embellishments.

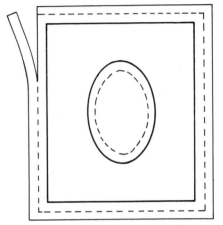

cut fabric 2 or 3 cm
(about 1″) larger than
wadded cardboard

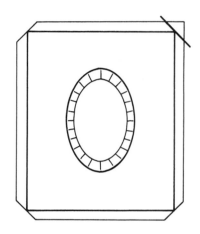

make small cuts around oval.
Mitre corners

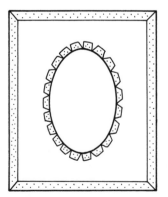

glue fabric to the back

Picture frame cover

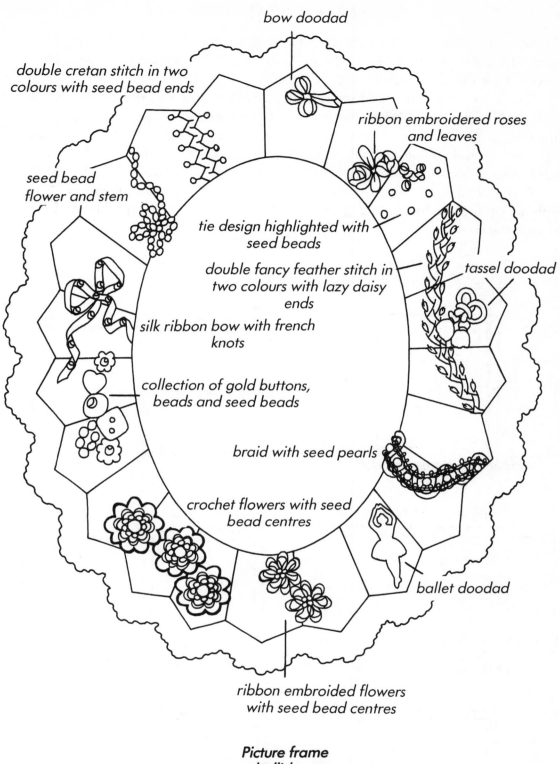

bow doodad

double cretan stitch in two
colours with seed bead ends

ribbon embroidered roses
and leaves

seed bead
flower and stem

tie design highlighted with
seed beads

double fancy feather stitch in
two colours with lazy daisy
ends

tassel doodad

silk ribbon bow with french
knots

collection of gold buttons,
beads and seed beads

braid with seed pearls

crochet flowers with seed
bead centres

ballet doodad

ribbon embroided flowers
with seed bead centres

**Picture frame
embellishments**

Photo album cover: Cut two pieces of wadding the same size as the front
and back of the album and glue in place. Open the album out flat and place
on top of the wrong side of the fabric. The crazy patchwork must be in the
centre of the front of the album. The back is covered in plain brocade. Cut
the fabric at least 2.5 cm (at least 1″) larger than the album all around. Make

a small cut in the fabric at either side of the spine, both top and bottom. Mitre the corners and glue the fabric down onto the inside front and back covers. Tuck the spine tabs in and glue down.

Cut two pieces of cardboard slightly smaller than the size of the inside front and back covers. Cut two pieces of plain brocade fabric 2.5 cm (1″) larger all around than the cardboard. Cover the pieces of cardboard, mitring the corners and gluing the fabric to the backs. Glue a tassel to the inside front cover. Glue the covered pieces of card to the inside front and back covers.

Cut a small oval out of the front and turn under a seam allowance. Slip a photo or picture inside and glue a narrow length of gold braid around the edge of the oval.

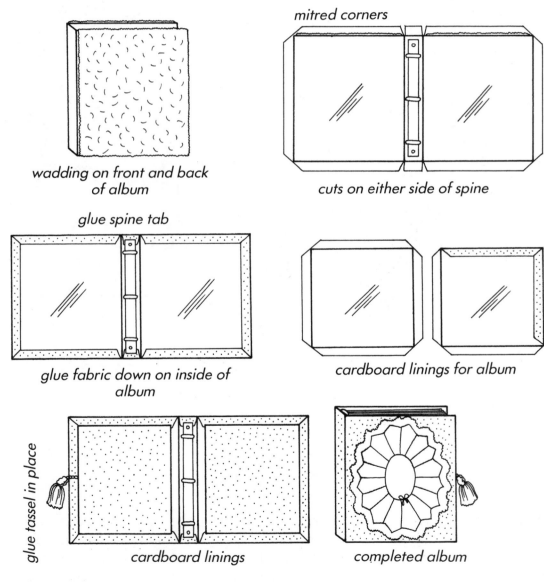

wadding on front and back
of album

mitred corners

cuts on either side of spine

glue spine tab

glue fabric down on inside of
album

cardboard linings for album

glue tassel in place

cardboard linings

completed album

Assembly of photo album

32

Photo album embellishment

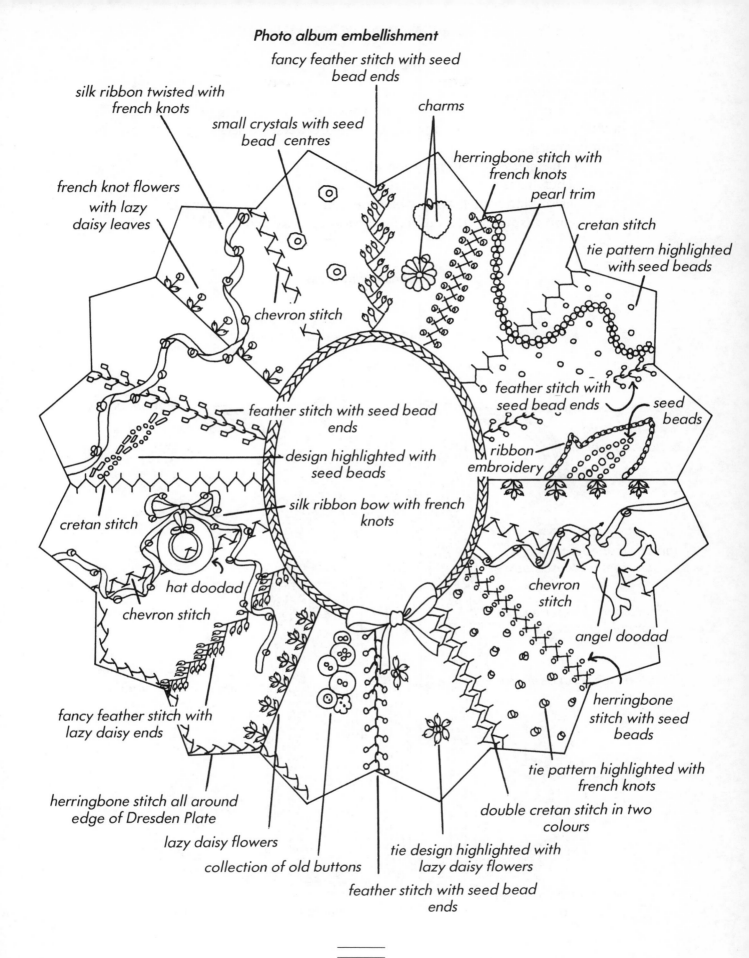

fancy feather stitch with seed bead ends

silk ribbon twisted with french knots

charms

small crystals with seed bead centres

herringbone stitch with french knots

pearl trim

french knot flowers with lazy daisy leaves

cretan stitch

tie pattern highlighted with seed beads

chevron stitch

feather stitch with seed bead ends

design highlighted with seed beads

feather stitch with seed bead ends

seed beads

ribbon embroidery

cretan stitch

silk ribbon bow with french knots

hat doodad

chevron stitch

chevron stitch

angel doodad

herringbone stitch with seed beads

fancy feather stitch with lazy daisy ends

tie pattern highlighted with french knots

herringbone stitch all around edge of Dresden Plate

double cretan stitch in two colours

lazy daisy flowers

tie design highlighted with lazy daisy flowers

collection of old buttons

feather stitch with seed bead ends

Christening set

Rummage through inherited or purchased old laces and fabrics to find keepsakes you can use to create this christening set as an original heirloom. The hatbox to store these beautiful pieces in between christenings tops off this stunning project.

All the pieces are a charming blend of old white, ivory and écru fabrics and crochet, tatted or embroidered lace. The dress and bonnet embody the principles of heirloom sewing, while the quilt and hatbox capture the Victorian love of embellishment in a different version of crazy patchwork.

Christening dress

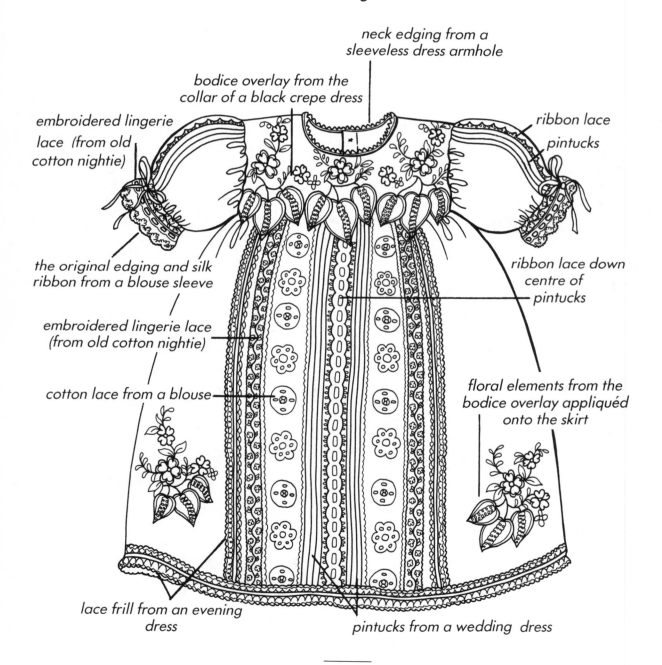

neck edging from a sleeveless dress armhole

bodice overlay from the collar of a black crepe dress

embroidered lingerie lace (from old cotton nightie)

ribbon lace pintucks

the original edging and silk ribbon from a blouse sleeve

ribbon lace down centre of pintucks

embroidered lingerie lace (from old cotton nightie)

cotton lace from a blouse

floral elements from the bodice overlay appliquéd onto the skirt

lace frill from an evening dress

pintucks from a wedding dress

M a t e r i a l s
• bits and pieces of old blouses, wedding dresses, debutante dresses, curtaining, lingerie, petticoats, rag bag scraps • Napisan to wash fabrics and laces • commercial pattern for a child's dress, petticoat and bonnet • cardboard hatbox kit • wadding • recycled buttons and ribbons • cream homespun • 1 cm (²/₅″) wide cream ribbon

I n s t r u c t i o n s

The purpose of these instructions is to show you how lots of different pieces of old fabric were combined to make items of clothing using a commercial pattern. Knowledge of actual sewing techniques is assumed; techniques are also described in the instructions that come with commercial patterns.

Sort out and mark all fabrics to be considered. Choose more than you need, to give yourself a wide choice when laying out the designs. Overlock some of the lace pieces together to reinforce the edges, as some old laces could otherwise disintegrate during handling. Wash all fabrics in Napisan or similar — this really brings them to life.

Christening dress: Choose the prettiest old fabrics and laces to decorate the christening dress. The one shown in the photograph was based on an old wedding dress which featured pintucks all the way down the front of the skirt. The pintucks again feature down the front of the christening dress skirt. Ribbon lace, unpicked from an old blouse, was stitched down the centre of the pintucks. Cotton lace from an old blouse was stitched on either side of the pintucks, and the next piece of lace came from a cotton nightie that had disintegrated with age, except for the lace. The frill on the outer edges of the panel and around the bottom of the dress came from an old evening dress — scorch mark and all.

The sleeves were made from the pintucks of the wedding dress bodice, again with ribbon lace stitched down the centre. Then came the lingerie lace, and finally the original edging used around the sleeves of the old blouse. The silk ribbon threaded through also came from the blouse.

The bodice overlay of the dress was made out of a collar on an old crepe dress. The floral elements in the collar were cut out and appliquéd as motifs on the dress and accessories, pulling the whole story together. The edging at the neck, which was kept intact, was originally an armhole edging on a sleeveless dress. The tortoiseshell buttons on the back of the dress came from a man's shirt. Wherever possible, the laces were joined up with small zigzag stitches, using silk embroidery thread in a Bernina overlocker, giving the whole dress a lovely heirloom look.

Petticoat: The basic fabric used was from a wedding train with a simple handcrocheted edge. Cotton lace around the sleeves and neck came from a petticoat. Appliquéd motifs on the bodice and along the bottom of the skirt were from a trim on a cream satin blouse; the same motifs were used on the quilt and bonnet. Press studs on the back were from a child's shirt.

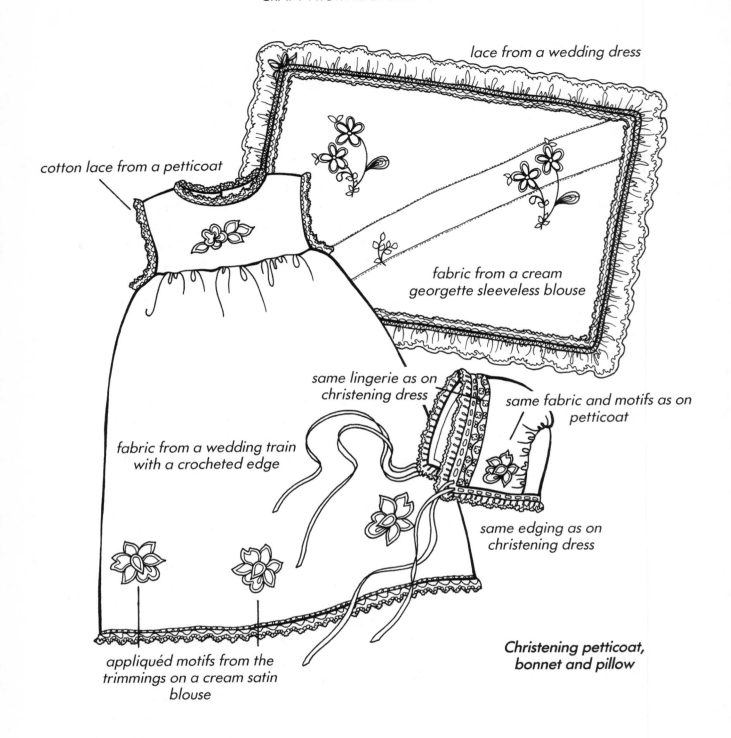

lace from a wedding dress

cotton lace from a petticoat

fabric from a cream
georgette sleeveless blouse

same lingerie as on
christening dress

same fabric and motifs as on
petticoat

fabric from a wedding train
with a crocheted edge

same edging as on
christening dress

appliquéd motifs from the
trimmings on a cream satin
blouse

*Christening petticoat,
bonnet and pillow*

Bonnet: The same base fabric and motifs as the petticoat were used for the bonnet. Bonnet edging came from the same lingerie lace and blouse trim as the christening dress sleeve.

Pillow: This was originally a cream georgette sleeveless blouse, the front and back of the blouse forming the front and back of the pillow. The lace around the edge came from a wedding dress.

Quilt: In many ways, the crazy patchwork technique used on the quilt is closer to appliqué than patchwork as the pieces were stitched onto a base fabric, not to each other. The raw edges of each piece were turned under or overlocked then pinned onto the base in such a way that it slightly overlapped its neighbours. No paper or templates were used, the shape of the pieces being dictated rather by the design of the laces. The individual pieces were anchored securely with different embroidery stitches.

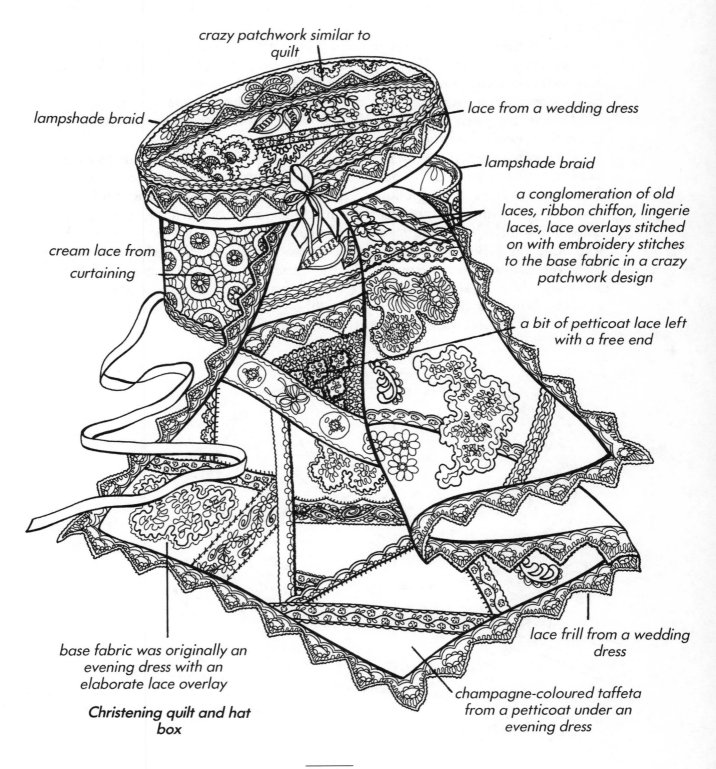

crazy patchwork similar to quilt

lace from a wedding dress

lampshade braid

lampshade braid

a conglomeration of old laces, ribbon chiffon, lingerie laces, lace overlays stitched on with embroidery stitches to the base fabric in a crazy patchwork design

cream lace from curtaining

a bit of petticoat lace left with a free end

base fabric was originally an evening dress with an elaborate lace overlay

lace frill from a wedding dress

champagne-coloured taffeta from a petticoat under an evening dress

Christening quilt and hat box

The back of the quilt started life as a satin blouse, which was cut into strips and restitched to form a rectangle the size of the quilt. A piece of Pellon wadding was placed on top of this backing, then a layer of champagne-coloured taffeta from the petticoat of an evening dress. The base fabric for the appliquéd pieces was originally an evening dress with an elaborate lace overlay. This cream lace overlay doubled, on the quilt, as a filler behind and around the patchwork pieces.

All the layers give the quilt a dimensional quality and a pleasing variety of colours.

The patchwork pieces used in the top layer are old laces, unpicked, washed and ironed before use. They came from the same lingerie, dresses, blouses and petticoats used to make the rest of the set, and some beautiful lace overlay blouses once worn over long black or navy skirts. Strips of white lace, probably old French, had been machine appliquéd with double herringbone brown and cream twin needle embroidery to create a strong colour contrast.

The patchwork pieces were laid onto the base fabric and moved around until the pattern created the best effect. Each piece was then tacked in place. Some of the laces were appliquéd on, others were left loose. The appliqué was worked with a combination of machine and hand embroidery. Hand embroidery included chain, feather and blanket stitches. Machine embroidery was done on a Bernina, using both twin and single needle techniques and many different stitches to complement the features of the lace designs. Machine embroidery can be so good that it is difficult to tell it from hand embroidery.

The bow was the last of the silk ribbon used on the christening dress. The lace frill around the edge was from an old wedding dress.

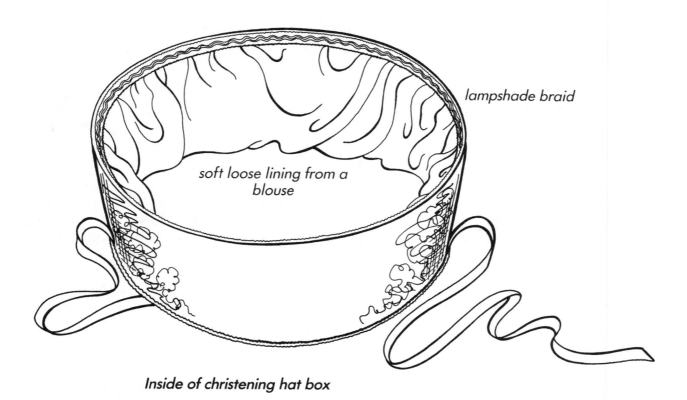

lampshade braid

soft loose lining from a blouse

Inside of christening hat box

Hatbox: The cardboard sides, top and base of the box are part of a commercial hatbox kit. All surfaces, both inside and outside, were covered with cream homespun as a firm backing, according to the kit instructions. The inside base of the box was padded before covering. The soft, loose lining of the box came from an old blouse. Braid from a lampshade was glued around the top of the inside wall to secure the lining.

Cream lace from some curtaining was glued on top of the homespun on the outside walls, and the overlap of the fabric was neatly concealed with another strip of cream lace. The lampshade braid was glued around the base of the box and around the top of the lid. The same lace as was stitched around the quilt was glued around the outside edge of the lid, and the top was padded according to the kit instructions. The top of the lid is similar to the quilt: crazy patchwork pieces, cut from the materials left over from the christening dress, appliquéd onto a base fabric made from a cream silk blouse. The base fabric was then glued down onto the wadded lid and the edges were finished off with more braid, with an extra strip across the lid. The final touch: ribbons to tie up the box.

Pillowcase doll

Made from a single pillowcase, this doll is very simple in construction with no facial features. The decorative Battenburg lace edge of the pillowcase was used as the main design of the skirt, and extra lace was added around the neck and sleeves to complement the skirt design.

As a transformed heirloom pillowcase, the finished doll — 50 cm (20″) long — is an attractive reminder of the Victorian era.

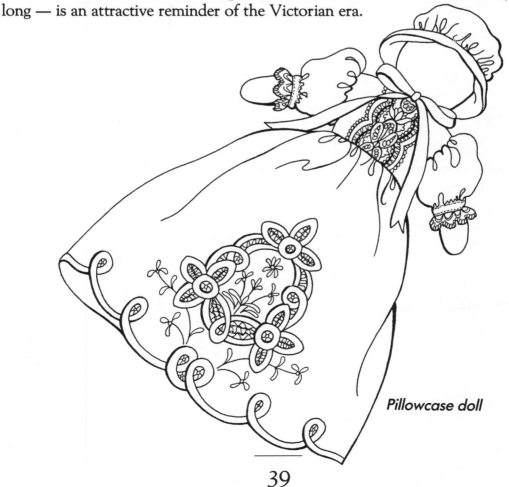

Pillowcase doll

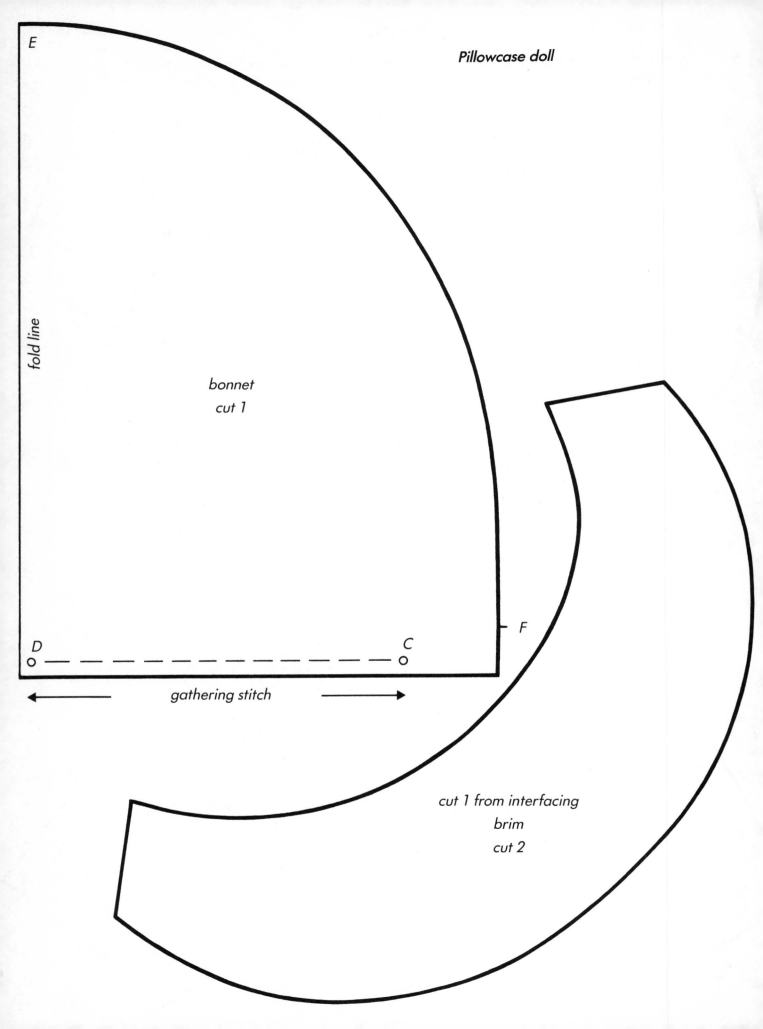

E

Pillowcase doll

fold line

bonnet

cut 1

D   C   F

○ - - - - - - - - - - - - - - - - ○

←   *gathering stitch*   →

cut 1 from interfacing

brim

cut 2

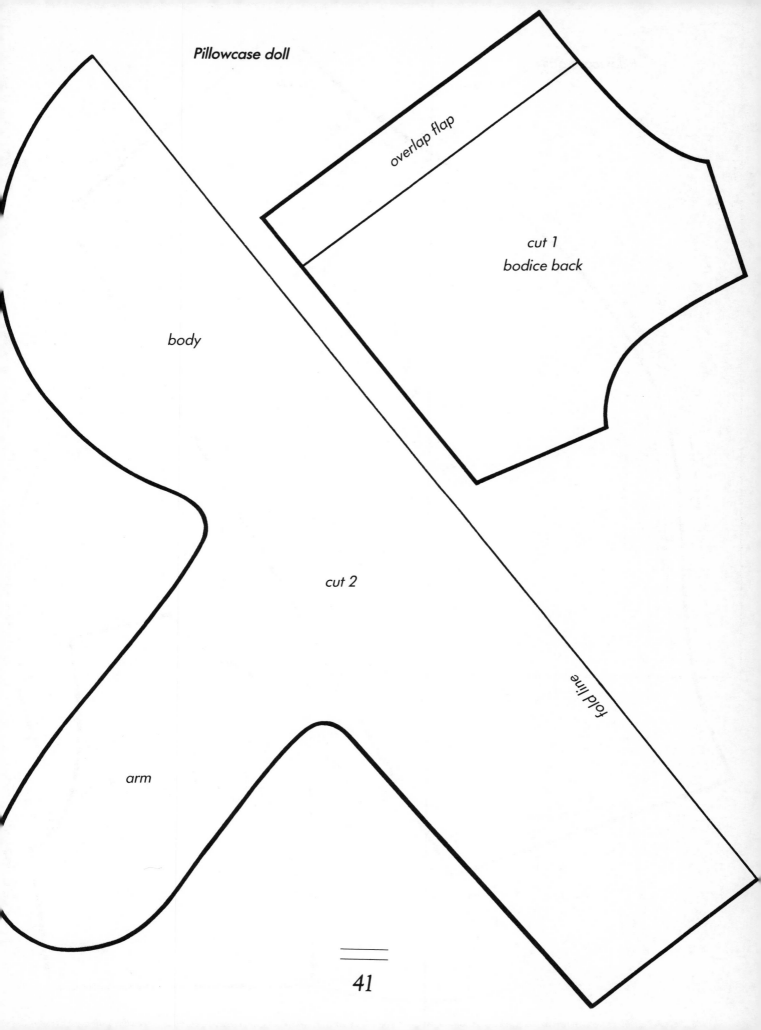

Pillowcase doll

overlap flap

cut 1
bodice back

body

cut 2

arm

fold line

41

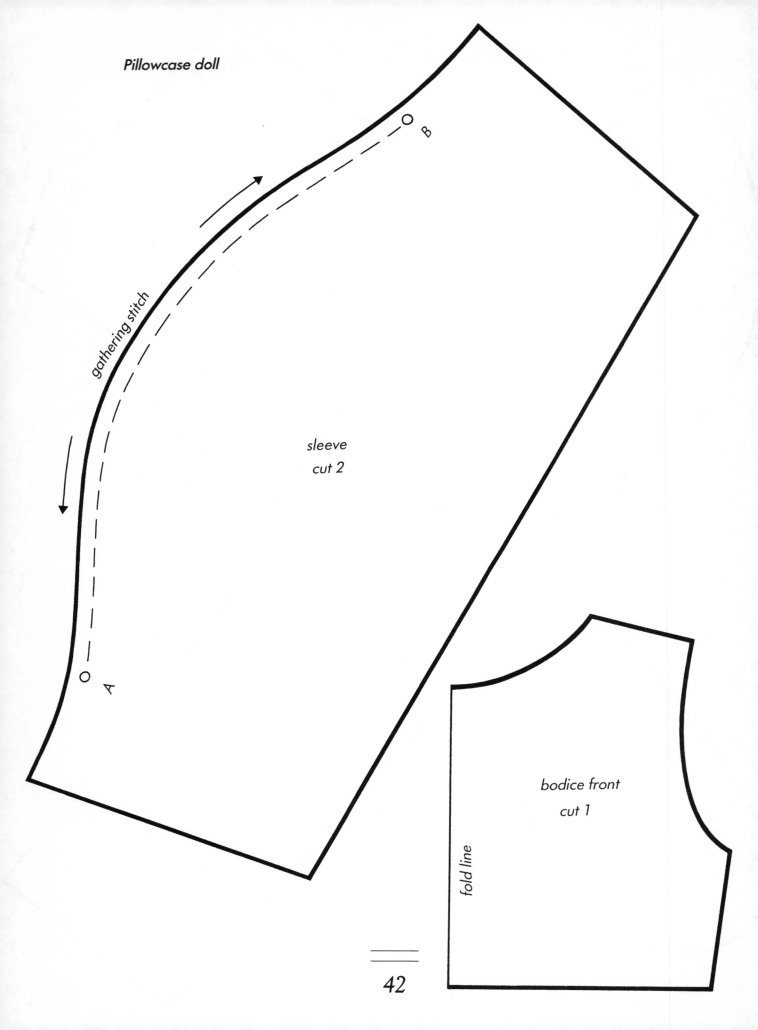

Pillowcase doll

B

gathering stitch

A

sleeve
cut 2

bodice front

cut 1

fold line

42

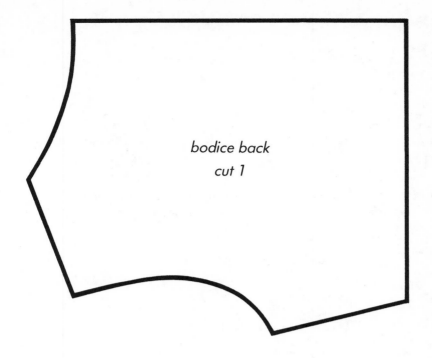

bodice back
cut 1

Materials

• *heirloom pillowcase with lace or embroidered border, 46 cm x 72 cm
(18″ x 28″)* • *10 cm (4″) fusible interfacing* • *stuffing — polyester
fiberfill* • *30 cm (12″) of white satin ribbon, 12 mm (½″) wide*
• *1 m (30″) of white lace, 20 mm (¾″) wide* • *10 cm (4″) of white
lace to feature on bodice front* • *30 cm (12″) of narrow elastic*
• *2 press studs*

Instructions

Cut off 36 cm (14″) from the open end of the pillowcase for the skirt and
use the rest for the doll's head, body and clothes. Trace the patterns onto
tracing paper and cut out each piece from the pillowcase fabric. Overlock
all raw edges. Use 6 mm (¼″) seam allowances throughout.

Body: Sew the right side of the body pieces together, leaving the bottom open.
Clip seam curves where necessary, turn right side out and press. Stuff the
head, arms and body firmly with polyester fibre. Slipstitch the bottom opening
closed.

Dress top: With right sides facing, sew front bodice to back bodice at shoulders.
On the right side of the bodice front, sew a strip of feature lace down the
centre. Sew gathering thread along curved top edge of sleeves between A and
B. Turn under a 10 mm (½″) hem along the bottom straight end of the sleeve
to form a casing for the elastic. Sew right side of lace trim to wrong side
of folded edge of sleeve. Gather top of sleeve. Measure a length of elastic
to fit around the doll's arm, including an overlap. Thread this elastic through
the casing, gathering to fit snugly around the arm. Stitch the overlap to secure.
Repeat for other sleeve.

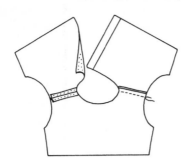

sew front and back bodice at shoulders

feature lace down centre of bodice front

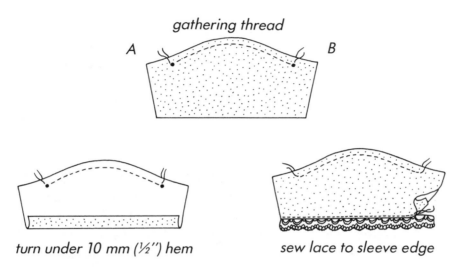

gathering thread

A   B

turn under 10 mm (½") hem

sew lace to sleeve edge

Pillowcase doll dress top

Sew the underarm and side seams in one continuous seam. Press the top of the dress. Turn right side out. Turn under the centre back bodice openings and sew. With right sides facing, overlock lace trim to neck edge, turning back a small hem at both ends of the lace. Turn lace right side up and press. Sew two press studs onto the overlap at the centre back opening.

Skirt: Sew a gathering thread around the cut edge of the pillowcase. Pull the gathers up to fit the bottom of the dress bodice. Turn the skirt wrong side out.

Place the dress top inside the skirt, with right sides facing and the raw edges of the skirt and top matching. Make sure the Battenburg lace on the front of the skirt is in line with the lace feature on the bodice. Attach skirt to top by sewing all around the raw edge. Turn completed dress right side out and press again.

Bonnet: On the bottom of the bonnet turn under 10 mm (½") hem. Press. Sew a gathering thread between C and D across the bottom of the bonnet. Pull the gathers up tightly and secure. Gather along the outer curved edge of the bonnet E to F.

Line the wrong side of one of the bonnet brims with fusible interfacing. Pin the two brims together, right sides facing. Sew around the larger outer curve of the brim and along the straight edges. Turn right side out and press. With right sides facing, line up the raw edges of the inner curve of the brim and the gathered outer curve of the bonnet. Sew, turn right side out and press. Cut satin ribbon in half and sew one length to each side of the bonnet.

Put dress on doll, add bonnet and tie on with ribbons.

Pillowcase doll bonnet formation

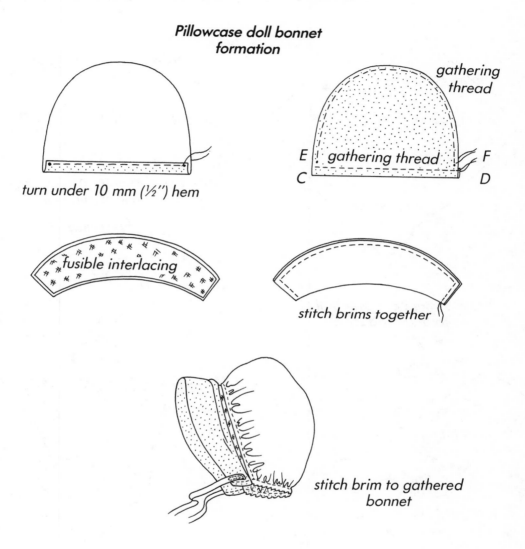

turn under 10 mm (½″) hem

gathering thread

E gathering thread F
C   D

fusible interlacing

stitch brims together

stitch brim to gathered bonnet

Handkerchief doll

This doll is an adaptation of the American 'church dolls', which mothers were said to have made by twisting hankies into imaginary figures to amuse their children while in church.

Old hankies with tatted or lace edging — which is often superb — can be turned into one of these dolls in just a few minutes. Optional additions include ribbons, bows, extra lace and flowers.

Materials

• embroidered or lace hankie • ping pong ball • needle and thread
• small artificial flowers • 1 m (30") of very narrow satin ribbon

Instructions

Follow the step-by-step diagrams to make your handkerchief doll.

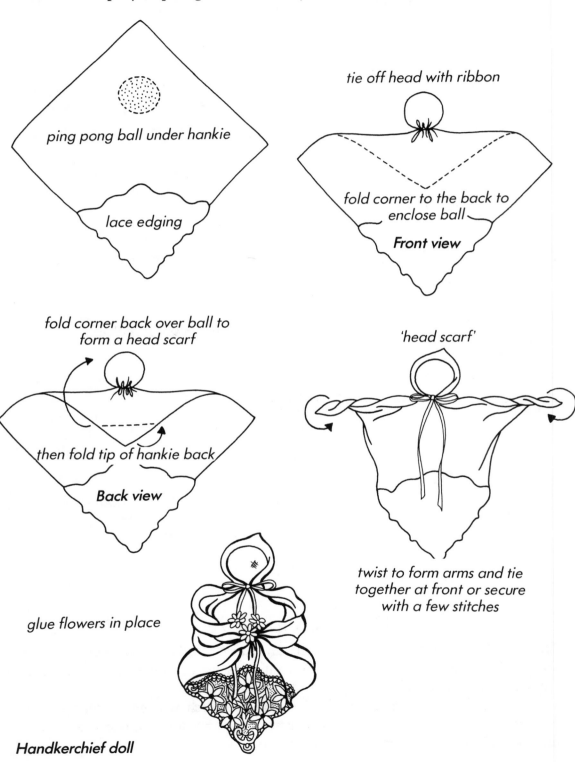

ping pong ball under hankie

lace edging

tie off head with ribbon

fold corner to the back to enclose ball

Front view

fold corner back over ball to form a head scarf

then fold tip of hankie back

Back view

'head scarf'

twist to form arms and tie together at front or secure with a few stitches

glue flowers in place

Handkerchief doll

RECYCLED DENIM

'The sturdy denim fabric was used by Levi Strauss & Co in the late 1800s to make "waist-high overalls" — or pants — for the miners of California. Denim clothing is to be found in the wardrobes of most households today. By the time the clothing is no longer fashionable or no longer fits, it has been washed and worn many, many times. A large quantity of denim is discarded, so over the past six years I have been collecting and recycling this softened and serviceable fabric. Family and friends now save their denim clothing for me, but this is not enough and I regularly visit secondhand shops and garage sales for additional supplies.'

Lyn Inall

General Instructions

Fabric: Collect all sorts of denim garments, in various conditions. Sometimes the knees of a pair of jeans are worn through but areas of denim faded in an interesting way, or attractive pockets and stitching, remain — all can be used to create texture and contrast in a project. Avoid using clothing made from stretch fabric or fabric which has been subjected to an acid rinse treatment, however. The stretch fabric will continue to stretch and the acid rinse fabric seems to wear into holes.

For added design interest, collect both patterned and plain denim clothing in all shades — light, medium and dark. The two colours found most frequently in denim clothing are indigo (blue) and black/grey.

Take down the hems of jeans and skirts if it looks as though there is an interesting pattern in the fading of this area, then wash everything.

Sewing machine: Most sewing machines will sew through several thicknesses of denim if they are correctly adjusted and serviced regularly, but check your machine before undertaking a denim collecting campaign.

Thread the machine with a good quality thread made with a polyester core and wrapped cotton.

Marking and cutting: Use white chalk, pastel pencil or a ballpoint pen to mark the shapes on the denim. A pen would generally not be used anywhere near fabric, but in the case of denim it glides over the fabric, including seams and pockets, and is easy to see.

Cut the marked shapes on the inside of the line. Since seam allowances are frequently included in pattern shapes, any marks remaining will be within

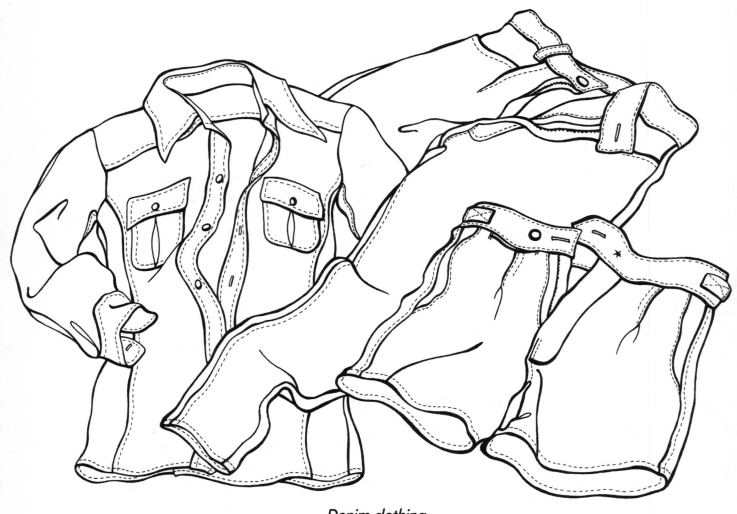

Denim clothing

these allowances. In the following patterns, the seam allowance used is the width of the presser foot on the sewing machine unless otherwise stated.

Converting denim clothing to reusable pieces of fabric requires a little thought. Cut jeans up and down the inside legs. Cut off the hems if they have not been let down before washing, and remove the zipper. Cut denim jackets along the the sleeve underarm seams and down the side seams. Unpick or cut down one side or centre back seam of denim skirts. Cut off the hem if it was not let down before washing.

Steam press everything out flat.

Denim bears

Recycled denim can be made up into cuddly, durable, soft bears. There are many teddy bear patterns available from specialty craft and patchwork shops as well as those available from major pattern companies and books. The bears shown in this book were based on McCall's Crafts pattern 2629 and Dream Spinners Bittersweet Bear pattern 114 by Great American Quilt Factory Inc.

Materials

• recycled denim • commercial teddy bear pattern • stuffing —
polyester fibrefill • thin interfacing or tracing paper • blunt stainless
steel knife • black embroidery cotton, buttons or bear eyes and nose
• optional: lace collars and doilies, ribbons, scraps of brightly coloured
fabric • lace fabric

Instructions

Follow the instructions given in the commercial pattern, taking note of the following hints and techniques.

Examine the individual pattern pieces and, wherever there is an area left open for stuffing, add a 15 mm (½″) tab to this area. This extra fabric in the seam allowance will make it much easier to pin and stitch the opening closed after stuffing the bear.

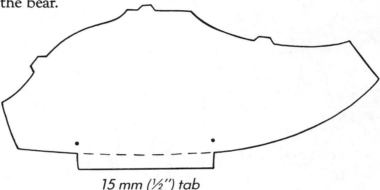

15 mm (½″) tab

Do not cut up the master pattern, which frequently includes several sizes and instructions. Trace the pattern pieces onto very thin interfacing or tracing paper. A pattern made from interfacing lasts for ages.

Before cutting out the bear, look for any interesting designs or features in the denim and place pattern pieces over these for maximum effect. Side seams of jeans, and striped, checked or spotted denim all add to the final result.

Use a smaller than normal stitch length when sewing curved pattern pieces together. This gives a smooth line of stitching with no need to lift the presser foot and move the fabric.

Where there is a sharp angle in a seam which has to clipped, reinforce the angle by placing a small scrap of fabric under this area and stitching through all the thicknesses. Go back and stitch a second row just in the angle area, alongside the first row but within the seam allowance.

second row of stitching

*reinforce the angle by
placing a small scrap of
fabric under the area*

Maurice

Martha

original jean seams

original jean seams

lace collar

jean pocket with stud

tartan bow tie

patchwork design of denims

patterned denim

original jean seams

denim bow tie

embroidered nose and mouth

lace doily

crocheted earrings

satin bow

half a lace doily

tartan scrap kerchief

jeans pocket with brand name tag

satin bow

gathered skirt from lace and pintucks

True Blue

Trudy

Denim bears

Use a good quality polyester filling with short, soft, springy fibres for stuffing the soft toys. Use a blunt stainless steel knife to help with the stuffing. If the bear is to be washed frequently, do not stuff it too firmly, but remember that the bear will last longer when firmly stuffed. Use very little stuffing where the legs join the body if the bear is to sit down.

To neatly stitch the opening closed, use a strong matching thread and ladder stitch. The stitches do not have to be close together; rather, stitch two rows — the first row up the back, the second row down the back, in between the first row of stitches.

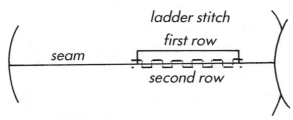

ladder stitch
first row
seam
second row

when the stitches are drawn together they sit in a straight line and close the opening neatly

Ladder stitching for opening

Embroidered eyes and nose are probably safer for small children, although buttons or bear eyes can be securely attached before the bear is stuffed.

Add extra embellishments as shown on the sketches.

Denim cushions

These three cushions — Blooming, Crazy Patchwork and Strip Pieced — each have different piecing techniques for the fronts but all use the same style back. The cushions are soft and very serviceable; they are well suited to a teenager's room, the family room, outdoor furniture, or a holiday cottage or van.

Materials
• *recycled denim* • *stuffing — polyester fibrefill* • *Grippers or zipper*
• *added fabric embellishments*

Instructions

Blooming cushion: This style (based on a technique from the Bloomin' Vest™ pattern by The Cambio) makes use of denim from the legs of various jeans in an unusual layering technique. First, cut off any bulky side seams, rejoin the fabric and press the new seams open. Cut five 45 cm (18″) squares of denim. As only the top layer will be visible, use the best piece of denim for this; the other four need not be so attractive, or can be much more worn.

With a pastel or chalk pencil, mark a 5 cm (2″) grid on the top square. The diagram also indicates the stitching lines. Place the five squares on top of each other with the grid square on the top. Randomly pin carefully through all five layers.

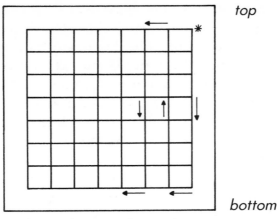

top

bottom

Blooming cushion

the grid square for stitching lines

Begin stitching down the right hand side of the grid, stopping at the corner but making sure the needle is left in the fabric. Raise the presser foot and turn the square. Stitch 5 cm (2″) to the next grid line, leave the machine needle in the fabric at the corner, raise the presser foot, turn the square and stitch to the top. When the stitching from right to left is completed, turn and come back using the same method, crossing over the already stitched grids. Continuing in this manner, it should not be necessary to end the thread until the entire grid is stitched. With sharp scissors, cut a cross in the middle of each square required to 'bloom'. Cut to within 10 mm (½″) of the stitching lines, and be sure not to cut the bottom layer of denim. If you do make a mistake, however, it is a simple matter to pin a patch to the back of the bottom layer and stitch around the small square, following the previous stitching line. The patch will be on the inside of the cushion and therefore not obvious.

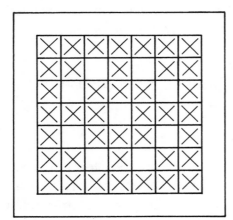

squares cut to 'bloom'

do not cut cross closer than 10 mm (½″) from rows of stitching

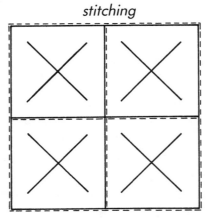

stitching

enlarged detail of squares

Make up cushion back as in instructions on page 56.

With wrong sides of cushion front and back facing, pin and stitch together, following the outside grid line. Stitch another row 8 mm (1/3″) outside the original grid and a final row 2 cm (3/4″) from the cushion edge.

Wash cushion and spin or line dry to achieve the 'blooming' effect.

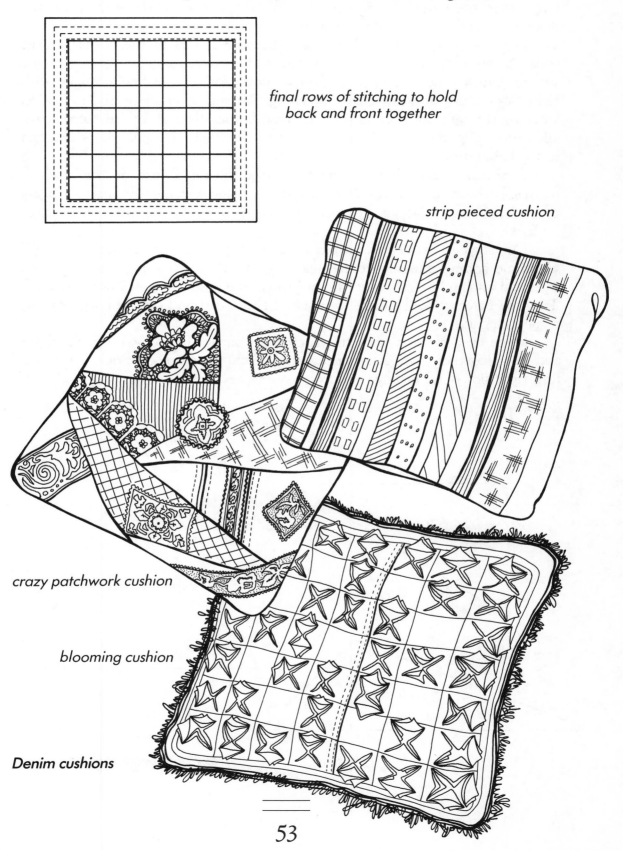

*final rows of stitching to hold
back and front together*

strip pieced cushion

crazy patchwork cushion

blooming cushion

Denim cushions

Crazy patchwork cushion: This is a good way to use up odd-shaped pieces of fabric. Each piece of fabric is cut into whatever triangular shape is needed to fill an area or continue a design — triangle types A, B and C. See the introduction to this chapter on page 25 for details about crazy patchwork.

Cut a square of denim, calico or medium weight scrap fabric, 10 cm (4″) larger than the required cushion size. This is the base fabric onto which the denim triangles will be machine stitched.

Beginning with a type A triangle (because it fills in the corner of the square), pin a triangle of denim so that it extends beyond one corner of the square. Cut a type B triangle and place it on top of the first triangle, with right sides facing and raw edges matching. Pin and stitch along the raw edge, stitching through both layers plus the base fabric. Trim away the excess seam allowance. Flip the second triangle over to the right side and press. Pin flat to the base fabric.

Lace can be added at this stage. Change the top thread on the machine to match the colour of the lace and attach using a decorative narrow zigzag or straight stitch. Tatting, crochet and old lace should be stitched in place by hand.

Cut a type C triangle and pin it to the top edge of the second triangle. Continue adding one shaped triangle after another, trimming, flipping them over and adding lace as required, until the entire base fabric has been covered. Trim the patchworked square to required size and round off the corners using a cup as a guide.

Make up a cushion back to match the front (see page 56). Pin the front and back together, right sides facing, and stitch. Zigzag or overlock the edges, turn right side out, pushing the corners out as neatly as possible.

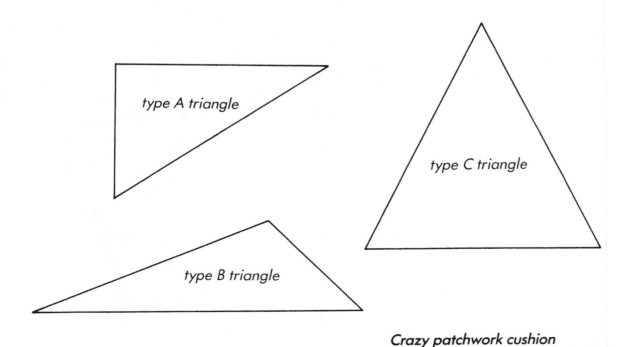

Crazy patchwork cushion

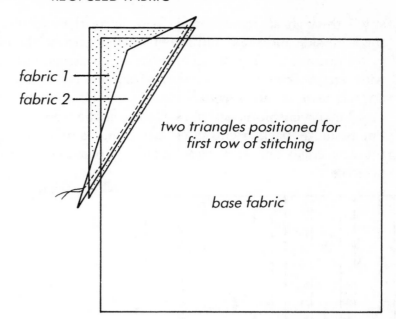

fabric 1

fabric 2

*two triangles positioned for
first row of stitching*

base fabric

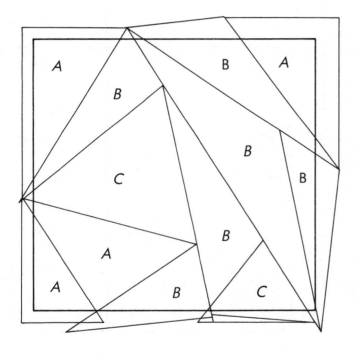

*one possible order of piecing
a variety of triangles*

*the square will be trimmed
to size when piecing is
complete*

Strip pieced cushion: Cut the denim into strips of whatever width is desired
— between 3 cm and 7.5 cm (1″–3″) looks best. If the strips are too short,
join two or more strips of similar widths, either straight or at an angle. The
combination of fabrics will add interest to the cushion.

Cut a base square of fabric a little larger than the required size of the
cushion. Arrange strips next to the base square into an attractive design,
beginning and ending with a wide strip. Take the first wide strip and pin it
in position along the left hand edge of the base square. Lay the second strip
on top of the first strip, right sides facing and raw edges matching. Pin and

stitch through all three layers. Trim away the excess seam allowance, flip to the right side and press. Pin the unstitched edge to the base fabric.

Continue adding strips until the base square is covered, ending with a wide strip. Trim the patchworked square to desired size, rounding off the corners using a cup as a guide.

Make a cushion back the same size as the front (see instructions following). Pin front to back, right sides facing and stitch together. Zigzag or overlock the raw edges and turn right side out, pushing out the corners as neatly as possible.

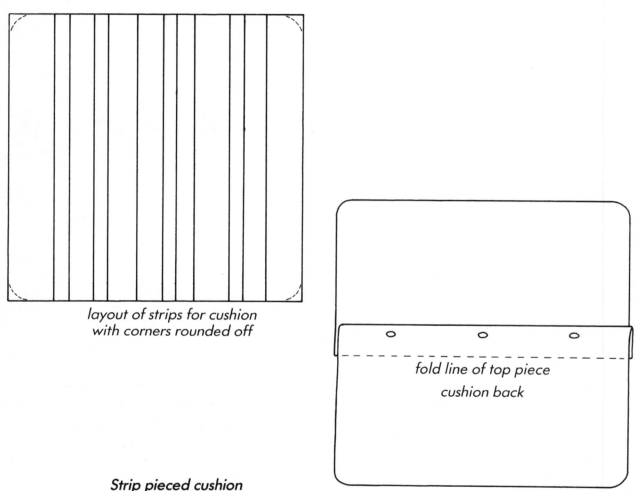

layout of strips for cushion
with corners rounded off

fold line of top piece

cushion back

Strip pieced cushion

Cushion back: The two pieces of fabric forming the back opening of the cushion need to overlap, and Grippers or a zipper are used to secure the opening. Grippers, the small tool needed to attach them and instructions are readily available in kit form from most haberdashery outlets.

Cut two rectangles of fabric equal to half of the cushion square plus 10 cm (4″). Zigzag or overlock the opening raw edges. Press 10 cm (4″) under as a hem on one rectangle only. Position the hemmed piece over the flat piece, overlapping them until they match the size of the cushion front. Attach a zipper or Grippers. The cushion back is now ready to stitch to the pieced front.

RECYCLED
bric à brac

RECYCLED JUNK

Junk wall hangings

'Our craft work is recycling with a vengeance, transforming yesterday's junk into today's treasures. Most of us don't stop and look at what is around us often enough.

This type of craft is challenging, constantly making you aware of your surroundings and forcing you to come up with new ideas for making use of those surroundings. We have often found it embarrassing scavenging around rubbish tips, gullies and old demolition sites, but each piece we find has a story to tell about where and how it became part of our creations.

Initially our craft work revolved around wreaths formed from recycled junk with tin cutouts in silhouette as the central theme. Recently we have diversified and are experimenting with some alternatives on which to mount our tin cutouts. These include long wooden boards from sheds, sieves, woodblocks, Singer sewing machine treadles, cogs from tractors, window frames, bike wheels and gates. The possibilities are unlimited, and in this way we have kept our work evolving and changing, no longer dependent on the wreath shape as a basis.

We always encourage people who buy our work to add to it themselves. Our pieces are not static in nature — each one has been created after many years of exposure to the elements. Just because we have collected a few of these weathered things and placed them together, it doesn't mean they should stop changing.'

Debbie Flannery

'When you're living off the land, everything possible is recycled from necessity. As a young child my creativity was stimulated by exposure to a number of wonderful old farm sheds, overflowing with an assortment of interesting objects of every shape and texture, just waiting to be transformed. When we had craft lessons at home, it wasn't using store bought paper and Textas, but old newspapers, bits of wire and string combined with items scavenged from those sheds, plus lots of imagination.

Now my work shed on our property at Murwillumbah is a collage of bits and pieces — sheets of tin, baskets of odds and ends, springs, rusty scissors, hinges off gates, bike parts, bits of mosquito net, clothes pegs, a variety of old bottles.

Recycling, whether from necessity or not, has made me aware of my surroundings — lovely forms, interesting knots of wire, twists of rope, the various shades of colour on the weathered and rusted tin. Not everybody sees these things.

When I'm assembling a wall hanging, the required piece of tin in specific colourings comes from a collection gathered on my travels. This type of recycling is giving old things another chance to be admired. The ordinary things, or the fragments of ordinary things, are being lost. They get thrown into gullies and tips, buried or ploughed into paddocks. It is nice to collect those little bits and pieces and use them in a different way so they can be admired again — recycling little pieces of history. Quite often, finding old things can make you stop and think about who may have used or loved them; for example, the treadle off an antique sewing machine puts you in mind of the lady who must have lived in an old cottage a hundred years ago, sewing for her children.

Learn to look for and collect interesting bits and pieces. When you recycle them, the trick is to get these things to go together.

Visitors who see my works are swept up in all the memories of those earlier days when my treasures were used as part of their daily lives.'

Sandra Flannery

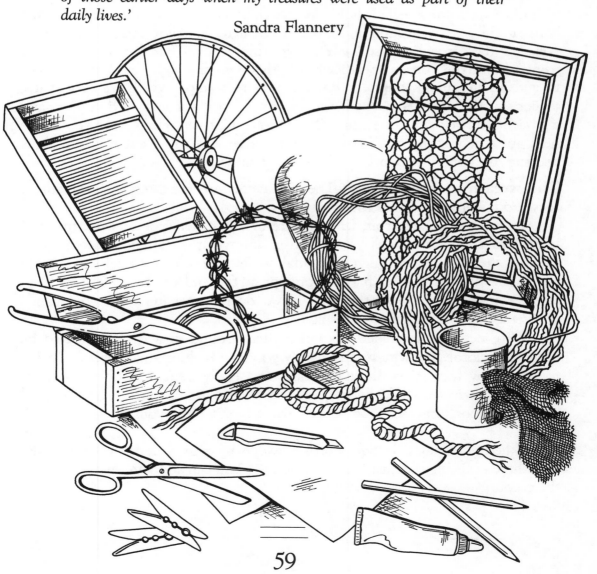

59

Instructions

Use anything and everything that appeals to you; it is all a matter of personal preference.

The sheet of tin: On a single piece of discarded tin, the subtle shadings can be beautiful, and the patterns that rust often creates are impossible to reproduce artificially. These colours may be related in part to the ageing of the paint, which gives gentle greens and sage blues through to pinks and a deep red oxide. It is extremely difficult to find matching rusts, therefore it is essential to maintain a fairly large collection to get the variety of colour.

The tin cutout silhouette: Drawing a silhouette is actually more difficult than drawing a detailed shape where you can add colour and distinctive features. Silhouettes really make you look closely at a particular object, to ascertain what is distinctive about it and then feature that particular quality without losing the shape's general look.

To make a basic silhouette use carbon paper and trace the shape onto cardboard. Cut a stencil of the design with a craft knife and lay it on the tin. This means you can see the desired area as the stencil is moved around until you find the colour variations to make the silhouette work. Even nail holes, if located in strategic places, can look effective.

Once you are satisfied, hold the stencil in place with spring clothes pegs and carefully draw around it. If the tin is light in colour use a black lead pencil; if dark in colour use a white colouring pencil. Then cut out the shape, using one of the cutters specifically for that job: the large ordinary tin snips to cut out the initial square of tin, and jeweller's snips, which are very sharp, to cut out the silhouette detail, using a curved pair for awkward corners and a straight pair for straight cutting. The cut must be very clean, with the blades held absolutely straight. Old tin tends to craze when you cut it at an angle, and the rust could break off, spoiling your final work.

The wreath or background: The silhouettes are mounted in a wreath of recycled material or onto a found object.

To make a wreath from fencing wire or any other type of wire, first roll it up into a circle much as you would a vine wreath, winding it around and around, then looping through the initial circle to hold it in place. Incorporate any interesting knots that may be present at the end of the wire. You need very strong hands to bend the wire. Never do this twisting while your hands are wet, otherwise blisters will result.

Wire netting, scrunched up and wound around in a circle, can also be used. Old clothesline wire is particularly good for making small wreaths, being found in lovely soft weathered colours and easily bent. Use found objects such as a chair seat, bike wheel, old washboard frame, picture frames, old cupboard door, dray seat, or barbed wire. Don't limit yourself to a wreath shape.

When choosing a background on which to glue your tin cutout, make sure there is visible contrast between the two. You can add wire netting behind the cutout.

Thread a length of wire across the centre of the wreath and glue the tin shape on to it using Selleys MultiGrip. Other glues may change the colour of the tin. Hold tin in place with spring clothes pegs until absolutely secure.

You can often put multiple tin silhouettes on the one work — two cats facing each other, a row of pigs, a line of goats, hearts or stars between the larger pieces.

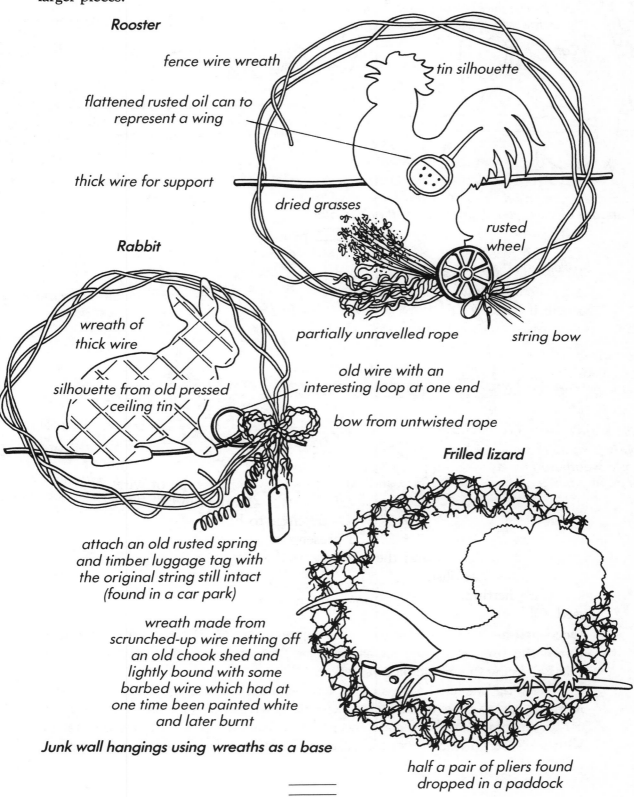

Rooster

fence wire wreath

tin silhouette

flattened rusted oil can to represent a wing

thick wire for support

dried grasses

rusted wheel

Rabbit

partially unravelled rope

string bow

wreath of thick wire

old wire with an interesting loop at one end

silhouette from old pressed ceiling tin

bow from untwisted rope

Frilled lizard

attach an old rusted spring and timber luggage tag with the original string still intact (found in a car park)

wreath made from scrunched-up wire netting off an old chook shed and lightly bound with some barbed wire which had at one time been painted white and later burnt

Junk wall hangings using wreaths as a base

half a pair of pliers found dropped in a paddock

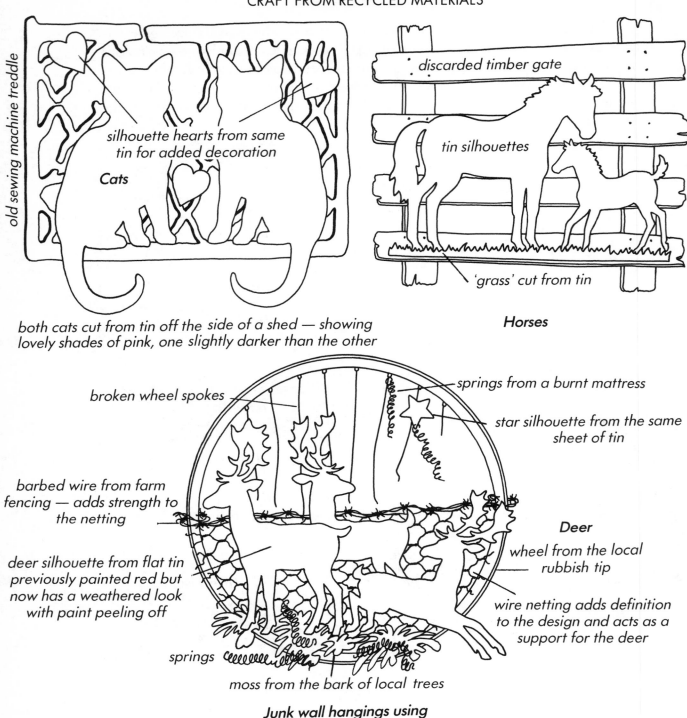

old sewing machine treddle

silhouette hearts from same tin for added decoration

Cats

both cats cut from tin off the *side of a shed — showing lovely shades of pink,* one *slightly darker than the other*

discarded timber gate

tin silhouettes

'grass' cut from tin

Horses

broken wheel spokes

springs from a burnt mattress

star silhouette from the same sheet of tin

barbed wire from farm fencing — adds strength to the netting

Deer

wheel from the local rubbish tip

deer silhouette from flat tin previously painted red but now has a weathered look with paint peeling off

wire netting adds definition to the design and acts as a support for the deer

springs

moss from the bark of local trees

Junk wall hangings using found objects as a base

Decorations: These works don't just happen, they take quite a lot of thought. Often the tin cutout will sit around for ages until you find just that thing that will bring the whole piece together.

Nothing is achieved if you purchase what is required. Try to gather related items to add to your work — for example, a wreath of wire with a tin rooster can be decorated with tin stars and gathered feathers, or a tin horse decorated with a discarded horseshoe, old rusty nails and a twirl of horsehair. Consider the colour, texture, shape, smell and visual aspects of the finished piece. Certain items will jump out visually as working well together. But don't clutter, because if the final piece is too busy it distracts from the tin cutout focal point.

Decorating does involve a lot of fiddling. Ribbons made from mosquito net and transformed into rag bows, shredded denim, rag strips of assorted fabrics from old dresses found in the charity shops, different coloured worn strings and ropes, or strips of old bandanas, can give the wreath that final touch. These additions blend in with the aged character of the craft work if they are torn, not cut into strips.

By untwisting rope you can get a kind of twirly length which also looks very effective.

Tin hearts are another form of decoration. Cut them out then punch 2 holes. The hearts should be cut at the same time as you cut the silhouettes otherwise it will be hard to choose sections that will blend with each other. Thread string or ribbon through these holes and tie around the wire.

Liquor decanter labels

When spring cleaning a dressing table drawer you may find some outdated spectacles. Have you ever thought to recycle the lenses as liquor decanter labels? Each lens can be handpainted with acrylic paints, mounted with jewellery findings and hung around the neck of your favourite decanter.

Materials

• lenses taken from old spectacle frames • very fine wet and dry sandpaper • acrylic paints: Wicker White (WW), Cherry Royale (CR), Bavarian Blue (BB), Sunny Yellow (SY), Thicket (T), Bayberry (B), Licorice (L) • waterbased varnish • brushes: 00 liner, No. 3 round, No. 1/4 deerfoot, No. 8 flat • grey graphite transfer paper • white tile palette • stylus or old biro • small gold cap jewellery findings • fine gold chain • clear craft glue • paper towelling

Instructions

Preparation: Use the wet and dry sandpaper to very lightly roughen the surface of the lens where the design will be painted. Wipe the lens free of dust.

Prepare the palette by mixing each of the specified acrylic colours with waterbased varnish in the ratio of two parts paint to one part varnish.

Painting the background: Pick up B on the dry deerfoot brush, then dab on paper towelling to remove excess paint. Holding brush in an upright position, pounce over the lens surface where the design will be, to form a soft background. Leave the centre of the lens unpainted. Allow to dry.

Repeat this pouncing with a little of the darker T to add contrast.

Design transfer: When the background is dry, transfer the design by slipping the graphite paper between the design and the lens, then tracing with a stylus. Alternatively, freehand paint the design referring to the pattern for assistance.

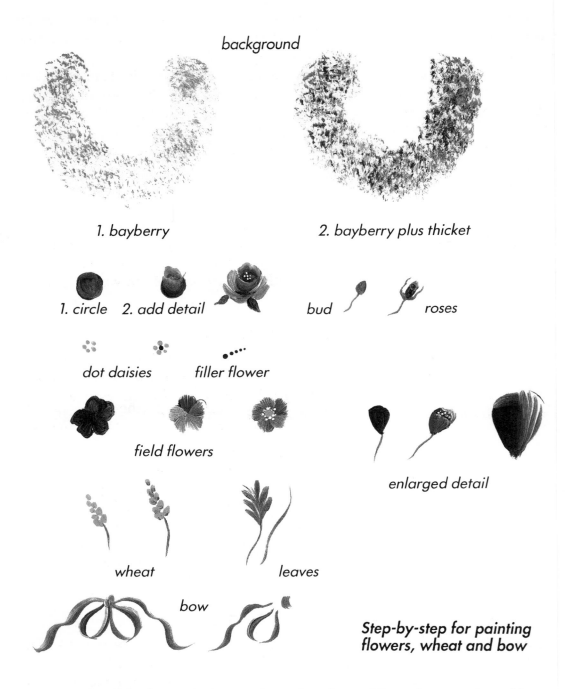

background

1. bayberry

2. bayberry plus thicket

1. circle   2. add detail

bud   roses

dot daisies   filler flower

field flowers

enlarged detail

wheat   leaves

bow

Step-by-step for painting flowers, wheat and bow

The whisky label: Load the 00 liner brush in BB and paint the ribbon, side load in WW and highlight the outside edge. Side loading is a technique for creating a blended stroke of colour by dipping one corner of the brush into the paint and stroking on the palette back and forth until this blended effect is achieved.

Use No. 3 round brush to paint circles of CR for the roses and smaller ones for the buds. Side load in WW, adding the comma-shaped petals as shown.

Daisies are added with five dots of SY and a central dot of CR. Dots are formed easily by dipping the end of the brush handle in paint. Clean and reload after each dot.

Filler sprays of flowers are smaller dots of BB made with the tip of the liner brush. Scattered WW dots form the remaining groupings of filler flowers.

The brandy label: Paint the ribbon the same as for the whisky label but using CR and WW.

Using No. 3 brush, base coat the field flowers in BB. When the first coat has dried apply a second coat. Load the liner brush in BB and side load in WW. Push the WW to the outside of the petals, then pull the WW down towards the centre of the flowers. This will give a streaking of white into the blue. With the liner brush add tiny WW dots to the centre of the buds and SY and WW to the open flowers.

The heads of wheat are painted in SY as a series of dots. When dry add tiny WW dots to highlight.

Using the liner brush, pull fine lines of T to form stems and grassy tendrils. The thicker leaves are painted as comma strokes of T tipped in WW. When tipping, load the brush in the initial colour then carefully place just the tips of the bristles into the second colour before commencing the stroke.

Finishing: Using the liner loaded in L, write the names for each label. It may be necessary to apply several coats.

When the paint has dried, use the flat brush to apply several coats of varnish over the painted areas, following manufacturer's instructions.

Attach jewellery findings and chain to each side of the lens with glue. Hang the completed labels around your favourite decanters.

field flowers and wheat

roses and rosebuds

Patterns for labels

BUTTONS

*M*ost housewives, crafters and avid collectors will have a button box — inherited, if you are lucky, from your mother or grandmother. In most cases, however, buttons are just accumulated during the course of everyday wear and tear — the inevitable lost buttons and buttons cut from clothing which has worn out, or is too small or no longer fashionable. Others have been bought from antique or opportunity shops and local markets.

This button collection can become the source of untold treasures if the humble button is viewed in terms of its creative potential.

A simple decorative feature can be made of the collection itself if the buttons are sorted according to colour and type, then stored in a few unusual old glass containers.

Buttons can also be recycled by co-ordinating the different styles and colours to make contemporary jewellery and hair accessories, by assembling them into a collage or by using them to add a unique touch to home decor and clothing items.

Compilation of things using buttons

HANDMADE PAPER: PAPER COLLAGE, GIFT BAG, GIFT BOX AND
PAPER SHEETS

RECYCLED TABLE LINEN AND TIES: LINEN BEAR AND SILK TIE PHOTO
ALBUM AND PICTURE FRAME

RECYCLED FABRIC: CHRISTENING DRESS, PETTICOAT AND BONNET, HATBOX, PILLOW AND QUILT

BRIC A BRAC: JUNK WALL HANGINGS

RECYCLED SPECTACLE LENSES: LIQUOR DECANTER LABELS

RECYCLED BUTTONS: BUTTON-TRIMMED CARDIGAN,
'HOLLYHOCK' GARDEN PICTURE AND TREASURE BOX

JUNK JEWELLERY: SOFT SCULPTURE HEART BROOCH, VICTORIAN
RIBBON ROSE BROOCH, BROOCH COLLAGE, BITS AND PIECES
BROOCH, CHARM NECKLACE AND LADIES TIE ACCESSORY

RECYCLED GLASS: DECOUPAGED PLATE AND A VARIETY OF
DECOUPAGED JARS, SMALL DECOUPAGED GLASS BOX AND IMITATION
STAINED GLASS JARS

RECYCLED CANS: TIN FILIGREE MIRROR FRAME, STRAWBERRY PAINTED
CAN, DECOUPAGED CANS, DAISY PAINTED CAN, TIN FILIGREE WALL
HANGING AND PIN CUSHION

RECYCLED LIGHT GLOBES: PAINTED CHRISTMAS DECORATIONS AND
MARBLED LIGHT GLOBES

'Hollyhock' garden picture

The buttons in this project were used to give texture and interest to a simple silk painted background. A selection of white and cream buttons were coloured with these silk dyes to give a compatible range of soft colours. The buttons will take up the dye to varying degrees depending on their individual composition, giving different shades of one colour.

Materials

- *assortment of old white and cream buttons* • *a piece of silk (Jap 10)*
- *timber screen or embroidery frame* • *drawing pins* • *white paper for the pattern* • *thick black pen* • *silk dyes in strong basic colours for dyeing buttons and painting the meadow flowers, and cream (background), green (leaves), yellow (flower centres)* • *small glass jars for the dyes* • *soft cloth or tissues* • *slotted spoon to remove dyed buttons* • *soft bristle watercolour brush* • *clear gutta* • *gutta nib and applicator bottle* • *white iceblock container to mix the silk dyes*
- *eyedropper* • *craft glue* • *a container for water to rinse brushes and for dilution of dyes* • *paper towelling*

Instructions

Dyeing: To dye the buttons, place them in a small jar with the chosen dye colour and a little boiling water. Leave for about half an hour, then remove and gently wipe dry with a soft cloth or tissue. Leave to finish drying on paper towelling

Background: Stretch the silk onto a timber screen and secure with drawing pins or stretch around an embroidery frame. The silk needs to be stretched evenly and as tightly as possible.

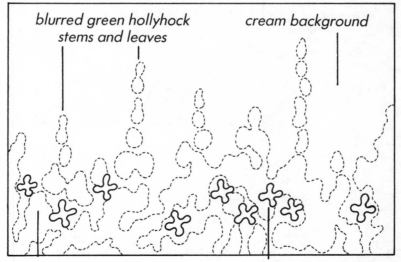

blurred green hollyhock stems and leaves — cream background

blurred green undergrowth — gutta meadow flowers

Silk painted background for hollyhock garden

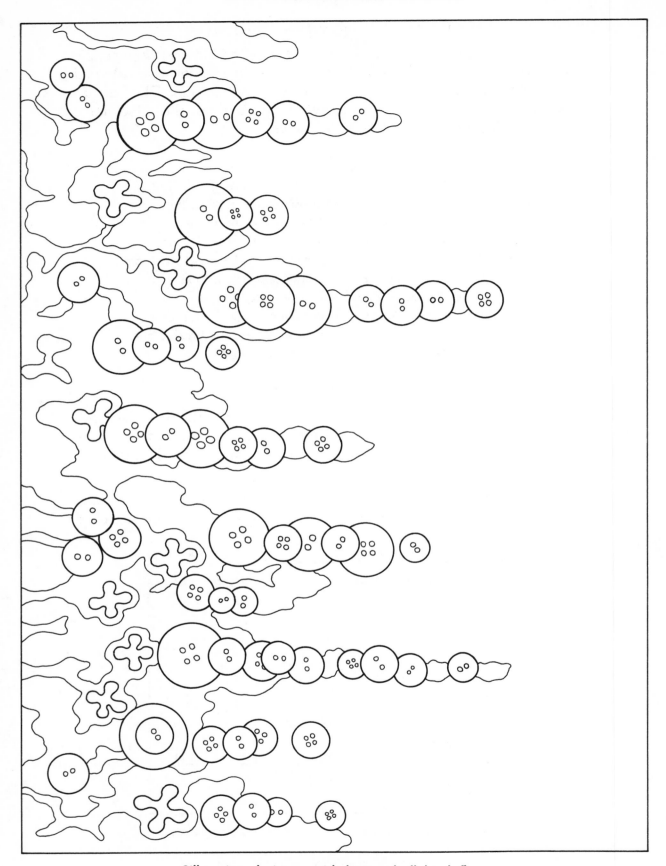

Silk painted picture with button hollyhock flowers

Draw or trace the design onto the paper with a thick black pen. Place this paper under the silk to act as a guide while painting.

On the silk, gutta in the tiny four-petal meadow flowers and a border indicating the outer border of the final picture. The gutta will form a barrier to the dye flow and is applied with a metal nib attached to an applicator bottle. Be very careful that there are no unwanted breaks in the gutta line as the dye will leak through and spread into other areas of the design.

Using a very diluted mixture of cream dye, paint in the background and around the flowers. Work quickly to get a uniform covering. While the background is still damp, place tiny spots of green to give the illusion of hollyhock stems, leaves and undergrowth. Without the confines of a gutta outline the green dye will spread to give a soft blurred effect.

With the brush, add a touch of the chosen dye colour to the top of each petal of each meadow flower. The colour will spread towards the flower centre. Place a tiny spot of yellow dye in the flower centre and this will spread outwards, blending with the petal colour. Leave to dry completely, then remove from the screen.

Finishing: Fix the dyes according to manufacturer's instructions.

Mount and frame the finished silk.

Arrange and glue the dyed buttons along the lengths of green dye to give the impression of hollyhock flowers and scatter a few amongst the meadow flowers.

Treasure box

Any uninteresting cardboard box can be brought to life by adding this silk-painted padded lid, where the flower texture is again achieved by the addition of dyed buttons.

M a t e r i a l s

The same as for the *Hollyhock garden picture* (page 67), plus:
- *old box* • *cardboard* • *wadding* • *scissors* • *strong craft glue*
- *acrylic paint to paint box* • *braid to decorate box*

I n s t r u c t i o n s

Background: Read silk painting instructions for *Hollyhock garden picture* (pages 67-9) before beginning. Prepare silk, trace the design and place under the silk to act as a guide while painting. Gutta the large flowers. Paint the background and around the flowers in diluted cream dye. While this is still damp, gently dab on the green dye between the flowers to form the background leaves.

Paint each large flower separately. Begin with one of the strong coloured dyes and paint around the edges of the petals. Put some yellow in the centre of each flower. Paint over the surface of both dye colours with water, blending softly with your finger to give a more subtle look.

Leave to dry completely, then remove from the screen. Fix the dyes according to manufacturer's instructions.

Dye the button selection in the desired colours as described on page 67. If desired, paint the box in a matching acrylic paint.

Padded lid: Cut a piece of cardboard and wadding the same size as the top of the lid. Cut the piece of silk 1 cm (½″) wider than this all the way around. Glue the wadding to the cardboard. With right side up, place the silk over the wadding, bringing the overlap to the back of the cardboard, and glue to secure. Pull the silk taut, mitring the corners and clipping where necessary to give a smooth finish. Glue the covered cardboard to the lid top, holding down with a few heavy books until dry.

Glue braid around the edge of the padded top, and around the bottom of the lid and the base of the box. On the centre front glue a figure eight in braid with a button in the middle.

In the centre of each flower, glue a selection of buttons dyed appropriate colours and grouped in a variety of ways to give texture and interest to the lid.

Pattern of flowers with button centres from lid of treasure box

Button-trimmed cardigan

Buttons can do much more than just hold garments together. Here is an idea to revitalise a plain cardigan by making a feature of some of the more unusual buttons found in your collection. When these are combined with simple wool embroidery, a unique look is created.

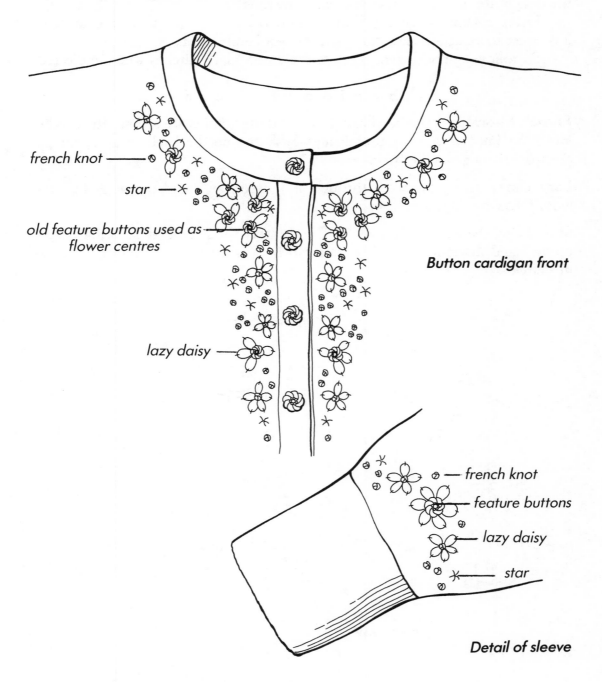

french knot

star

old feature buttons used as
flower centres

lazy daisy

Button cardigan front

french knot

feature buttons

lazy daisy

star

Detail of sleeve

M a t e r i a l s
• *plain angora cardigan* • *tapestry needle* • *12 feature buttons for design* • *cotton* • *tapestry wools: sandstone (S), light apricot (LA), dark apricot (DA), dusty green (DG)* • *tracing paper* • *large pins*

Instructions

Enlarge and trace both sides of the sketch design for the cardigan front and that for the sleeves. Tack the tracing paper in place and mark with pins the main elements of the design. It is impossible to attempt to mark the position of all the smaller details. These should be stitched freehand by referring to the design. Remove the paper and leave the pins.

Using cotton, stitch the buttons into position. Once these are in place it is easier to visualise where to begin the wool embroidery.

By following the design, recreate the embroidery stitches where indicated.

Embroidery Guide

French knot: Bring the needle up at 1, wind the wool twice around the needle. Hold the knot with your thumb and push the needle back in at 2, pulling the wool through to the back.

Lazy Daisy: Bring the wool through at 1, insert at 2 and out at 3. Pull the wool through and insert again at 4.

Star: Bring the needle through at 1 and insert the needle at 2. Bring needle up at 3 and insert again at 2. A star can be formed by arranging the stitches in a circle.

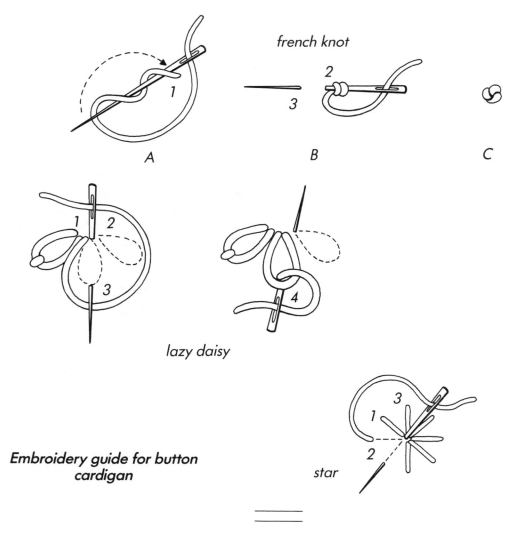

Embroidery guide for button cardigan

JUNK JEWELLERY

Turning junk or ordinary bits and pieces into unique and beautiful jewellery always offers a creative challenge. Scrounge around garage sales, collect your own and any other person's broken costume jewellery or watch parts, bits of lace, doilies, ribbon and braid, old buttons, beads and pearls. Often these materials have a sentimental value and the resultant item of jewellery becomes a keepsake of that special memory. Likewise, it may have an antique quality to it reminiscent of the opulent Victorian era.

A variety of things can be used as a base, such as a piece of felt, an old tie or large button, a padded cardboard shape, a length of necklace chain or flattened piece of oven-bake clay. Of course these are just a few possibilities; your exploration of alternatives is limited only by your imagination.

Victorian ribbon rose brooch

Materials

- 40 cm (16") of 35 mm (1½") wide wired apricot ribbon
- 50 cm (19") of 35 mm (1½") wide wired rose red ribbon
- 30 cm (12") of 35 mm (1½") wide wired green ribbon
- small lace doily • bead and net hat trim • glue
- 5 cm (2") square of felt or leather • brooch finding

Instructions

Gather along one side of the length of apricot ribbon. Form a 'rose' by rolling the ribbon from one end, while holding the gathered edge with your fingers. Open out the flower and press flat, securing the circle at the back with glue. Frill the wired edge to give a realistic look. Repeat for a second 'rose' with the red ribbon.

Cut three 9 cm (3½") lengths of green ribbon to form the leaves. From a point at the middle of the length, fold one half diagonally towards the back and one half diagonally to the front. Gather in at the base of the leaf and glue. Repeat to make another two leaves.

Cut a small square of felt or leather for the backing. Glue the two roses onto the backing so that they are overlapping each other, then glue on the three leaves and the net, beads, and doily embellishments.

Glue a brooch finding to the back.

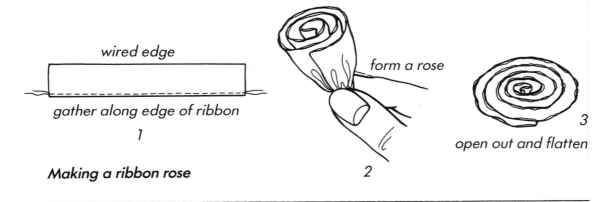

wired edge

gather along edge of ribbon

1

form a rose

2

open out and flatten

3

Making a ribbon rose

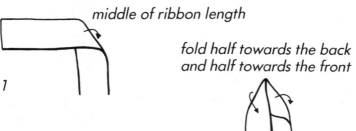

middle of ribbon length

fold half towards the back
and half towards the front

1

2

3

gather in the base of the leaf

Making a ribbon leaf

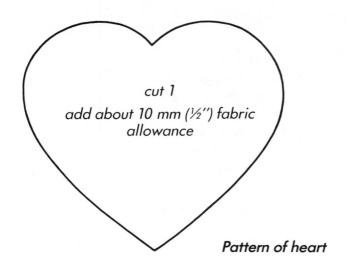

cut 1
add about 10 mm (½″) fabric
allowance

Pattern of heart

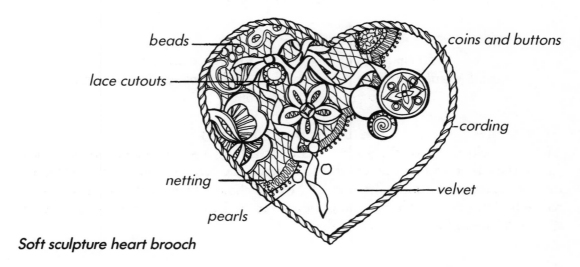

beads

lace cutouts

netting

pearls

coins and buttons

cording

velvet

Soft sculpture heart brooch

Soft sculpture heart brooch

Materials
• *silk velvet • cardboard • wadding • spray adhesive*
• *glue • embellishments such as old lace, braid, tiny bows, pearls,*
buttons, beads • brooch finding • narrow cord • felt

Instructions
Cut a small heart shape from cardboard. Glue some wadding, the same heart shape, onto one side of the cardboard with spray adhesive. Cover with silk velvet that has been cut about 10 mm (½″) larger than the cardboard. Using clear craft glue, wrap this allowance onto the wrong side of the heart and glue.

Decorate the front of the padded heart with old lace, braid, a tiny bow, some pearls, buttons or beads.

Glue narrow cord around the edge of the heart to conceal the seam.

Glue felt to the back of the heart and attach a brooch finding.

Brooch collage

Materials
• large button for base • brooch finding • bits and pieces for collage
such as buttons, charms, studs, buckles • glue

Instructions
Select a fairly large button as a base for the collage. Glue the flat buttons on first to cover the base. On the top layer, glue the feature charms, studs, buckles and any other embellishments.

Glue the brooch finding to the back of the base button.

Charm necklace

Materials
• 50 cm (20″) of strong chain • necklace findings
• small metal jump rings • 'charms' such as old drop earrings, lockets, charms, beads, coins

Instructions
Make a necklace from the strong chain, attaching a strong catch on one end. Leave the other end so the length of the necklace can be adjusted for different outfits. Across the middle 25 cm (10″) of the chain join any interesting 'charms' to each chain link with the jump rings. Put at least one charm on each link for a full, heavy look.

Ladies' tie accessory

Materials
• old tie • used curtaining • iron-on interfacing • embellishments such as old doilies, pieces of lace, fine chains, a tassel, some old buttons, ribbon roses, leaves

Instructions
Using an old tie as a pattern, cut a tie shape from the curtaining fabric. Add a 6 mm (¼″) seam allowance. Cut some iron-on interfacing the same shape as the tie and fuse to the wrong side of the fabric.

Sew up the tie, slipstitching the seam down the centre back.

Trim the bottom of the tie with the old doily, extra lace, chains, a tassel, some old buttons, roses and leaves (see 'Victorian ribbon rose brooch').

Bits and pieces brooch

M a t e r i a l s

• *oven-bake clay (Fimo)* • *metal embellishments such as assorted findings, stampings, jewellery bits, charms, glass stones, beads* • *wire cutters* • *spray varnish* • *bronzing powder* • *brush* • *dark brown acrylic paint* • *two-part epoxy glue* • *lint-free cloth* • *brooch finding*

I n s t r u c t i o n s

Roll out a 3 mm (¹⁄₁₀″) thick piece of clay as a backing for the brooch. Press the metal embellishments into the clay in an interesting arrangement. Add some clay cutouts if desired.

Cut the attachment rings off the charms with wire cutters or use the rings as attachments for chain tassels.

Bake the clay in the oven according to manufacturer's instructions. After this it may be necessary to glue some of the embellishments back in place.

Spray the brooch with varnish. While it is still wet, brush bronzing powder over the surface, avoiding the stones. Spray again with varnish to seal the powder.

To antique the brooch apply some dark coloured paint all over, especially in the grooves. Quickly wipe off the excess paint with a lint-free cloth, leaving sufficient in the grooves to give an old world look. Spray again with varnish.

Scratch the back of the brooch where the finding is to be attached. Glue the brooch finding on using the two-part epoxy.

RECYCLED
cans

*E*very year, billions and billions of empty cans are tossed onto rubbish tips. If cans, regardless of size, were recycled it would be a big step towards reducing the damage to the countryside caused by mining the raw materials needed to make them. As in most industrial processes, there is also a certain amount of chemical waste released which in turn pollutes the soil and river systems. Stop and consider these cans not as throwaways but as raw materials for craft projects. You can decorate them with painting or découpage, or cut them up to represent 'iron filigree' — and the results will be well worth keeping for yourself or giving as gifts. Old tins can be cleverly converted into simple pincushions, useful canisters for tea bags or freshly ground coffee, pen and pencil holders. They can be cut and twisted to form intricate filigree work to frame a mirror or to use as a 'Spanish' wall hanging.

'To make something both beautiful and practical from so-called "rubbish" is always a satisfying challenge. It is such a pity that we throw so much material away when it could be used again. Nature recycles everything so why can't we? People really admire ingenuity, and as this is such a throwaway society it is refreshing to see intelligent people really thinking about what they can do. Maybe this is a positive side of an otherwise depressed economy throughout the world.'

Anne Colligan

*Raw materials for
decorative painting on cans*

Decorative Painting on Cans

Decorative painting on tin cans can give them a totally different look the second time around. Turn them into containers to hold pens, potpourri, odds and ends, tea bags or ground coffee, stuffed to make a simple pincushion or filled with homemade goodies from the kitchen.

Materials

• small cans (in examples cans for camembert cheese, Carnation milk were used) • medium can (in example Milo can was used) • Jo Sonja acrylic paints: black (B), white (W), plum pink (P), red earth (RE), french blue (FB), aqua (A), raw umber (RU), jade (J), red oxide (RO), pine green (PG), Turner's yellow (TY), napthol red light (NRL), moss green (MG), gold (Go), burgundy (Bu) • Rowney No. 3 paint brush • Raphael No. 4 liner brush • small flat brush • stiff bristle brush for stippling • white tile as paint palette • mineral turpentine • abrasive liquid cleanser such as Jiff or Ajax • scourer • water based sealer • water based varnish • sponge brush for applying sealer, base coats and varnish • white carbon transfer paper • tracing paper • white chalk • eraser

Extra materials for pincushion: • cardboard • stuffing • fabric • glue

General Instructions

Preparation of cans: Soak cans to peel off labels. Remove any label adhesive with mineral turpentine. Using the abrasive cleanser on a scourer, scuff up the surface. Rinse thoroughly with 50/50 water and vinegar solution. Dry completely, especially inside the can. If you're in a hurry you can use a hairdryer, but be careful as the metal surface may become hot.

Brush on two thin coats of sealer inside and out, drying well between each coat.

Mix B with sealer 50/50 and base coat the tin inside and out. When dry repeat with another coat. Set can aside for a few days until paint has cured.

Pattern transfer: Transfer the pattern to tracing paper and tape into position around the tin, making sure the metal seam is at the back of the can. Be very careful as the paint could lift off with the removal of the tape unless it has cured properly. Place carbon between the can surface and tracing paper. Trace the pattern onto the metal surface.

Pincushion

Use a can such as one for camembert cheese. Transfer pattern onto can as described previously or if you prefer paint can freehand as follows. Mark can just under the rim every 3 cm (1¼″) with white chalk. Paint in W dots over these marks and repeat them around the bottom of the can. Dots can be made easily by dipping the end of the brush handle in the paint. Clean and reload after each dot to ensure that all dots are the same size.

Lightly mark crosses between the upper and lower dots and go over them with thinned W paint. The stroke should be narrow at the beginning and end but widen in the centre. Place a P dot in the centre of each cross and surround it with five W dots.

When the paint is thoroughly dry, remove any chalk marks with an eraser. Apply two coats of water based varnish, following manufacturer's instructions.

Cut a circle of cardboard to fit loosely inside base of can. Cut a circle of fabric 15 mm (⅝″) larger than the cardboard. Place filling material between cardboard and fabric. Place fabric over the filling and glue under the cardboard. Slip this cushion inside the can.

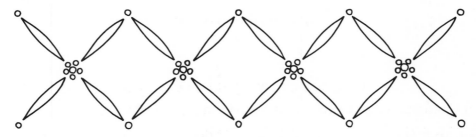

Pattern for can pincushion

Daisy painted can

Transfer pattern onto can as described previously.

Leaves: These are painted with two large comma strokes using a mixture of J, RU and A. The commas begin at the leaf base and finish at the tip.

Stems and tendrils: Paint in the same mixture as the leaves, using a liner brush.

Daisies: Load brush in W and paint petals with large comma strokes pulled towards the flower centre. Centres are a circle of FB, covering over the comma stroke tails. Highlight is a side load of W applied in a crescent stroke while the FB is still wet. Side loading is a technique for creating a blended stroke of colour by dipping one corner of the brush into paint and stroking back and forth on the palette until a blended effect is achieved.

Place random large and small W dots around lower rim of FB centre.

Fillers: Scatter W dots in groups of three.

Finishing: Paint top and bottom rim in RO.
Rub out carbon marks and apply two coats of varnish.

Pattern for daisy can

Strawberry painted can

Transfer pattern part 1 onto can as described previously.

Leaves and stems: Paint in PG as in *Daisy can*, then over the top of this paint with PG and MG.
Tendrils and stems are painted with the same mix, using a liner brush.
Transfer pattern part 2 over pattern 1, matching the centre line.

Flowers: Load one side only of small flat brush with TY and MG mix, then pick up W on the same side. Paint flower petals, keeping the texture to the outside edge with little or no paint in the centre of the half circle strokes. Fill in flower centres with MG. Scatter large and small dots in both W and TY around the centres.

Small strawberries: Base strawberries in TY and MG mix using shape following strokes. While still wet side load brush with NRL and paint just on outside of each berry.

Large strawberries: Paint base coat in TY and MG mix as for smaller berries, then paint with NRL. Shade lower edge of berries in a NRL and PG mix. The hull comma strokes are a mix of PG and MG. Seed pockets are placed on next as tiny B dots with TY highlights.
Using a dry, stiff bristle brush lightly dipped into W, stipple highlights on each strawberry. To stipple, load the brush with paint, dab out a proportion onto paper towelling. Then holding the brush in an upright position, pounce the bristles up and down over the area to be painted.

Finishing: Paint a fine Go line around the edge of the inner circle of the lid with a liner brush. Place narrow masking tape around the top and bottom edge of the can. With a liner brush paint in Go stripes using the tape as a guide line. Paint top and bottom rim in Go. Paint in Go highlights over tendrils.

When dry, rub out all carbon lines and apply two coats of varnish.

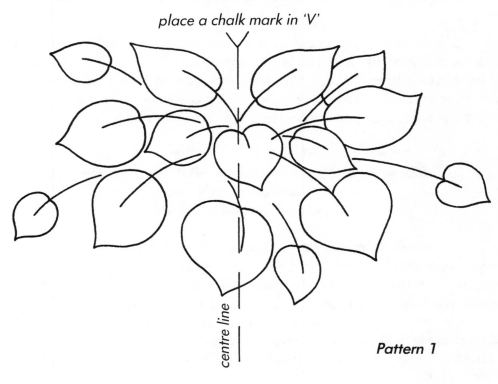

place a chalk mark in 'V'

centre line

Pattern 1

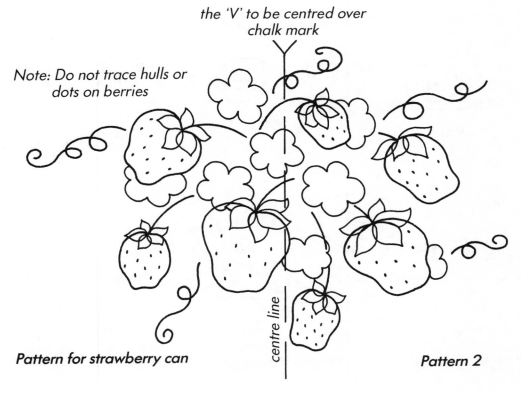

the 'V' to be centred over chalk mark

Note: Do not trace hulls or dots on berries

centre line

Pattern for strawberry can

Pattern 2

IMITATION IRON FILIGREE

*T*hese pieces of imitation iron filigree started as cans of all shapes and sizes, stripped of their labels and cleaned. When cut into strips, twirled and bent into filigree shapes with pliers and sprayed with black, gold or silver paint, they certainly make interesting conversation pieces indoors or outside. Display them in a safe position as the edges are quite sharp.

Materials
• *thick gardening gloves* • *tin snips* • *metal ruler* • *marking pen*
• *assorted clean cans* • *metal glue* • *mirror*
• *spray paint: black, silver, gold*

General Instructions
Always wear gloves to protect your hands from the sharp edges of the can. Using the tin snips, cut all the cans down their seams to open them out. Remove the outer raised rims so a piece of flat metal is left.

Mark equal strip widths along the length of the can using a metal ruler and marking pen. With the tin snips cut out all the marked strips.

Take a close look at the pattern and decide which shapes are going to be appropriate.

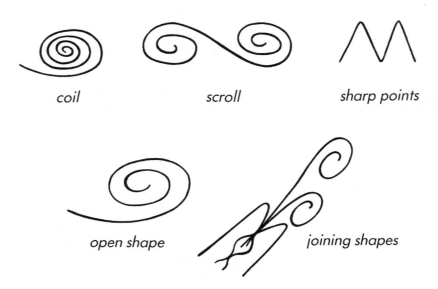

coil   scroll   sharp points

open shape   joining shapes

Filigree shapes

Filigree Shapes

Coil: Grasp strip near the end with the snips and turn metal in a circle around a suitably sized object to form a tight coil.

Scroll: Form a coil at both ends of the strip, either facing each other or going in opposite directions.

Sharp points: These are formed when the strip is bent over a thin metal ruler or bent by carefully pinching the strip at the exact point required.

Open shapes: Any of the filigree shapes can be opened out by gently pulling the coil.

Joining shapes: Strips are joined together with a metal glue.

Mirror frame

Measure a mirror, divide the dimensions into equal parts of approximately 2.5 cm (1″). Make enough scrolls to go all around the perimeter. Complete six hearts by bending strips in the middle and at each end form two coils facing each other.

Place on mirror to check fit. Relocate on a sheet of newspaper. Join all the parts together with a tiny dob of glue. Leave to harden. Spray with paint from all directions to ensure total coverage. When dry give a second coat if necessary. Leave for 48 hours. With a clear adhesive, glue the filigree around the mirror.

Pattern for filigree mirror frame

**Pattern for filigree turkey
wall hanging**

Wall hanging

Enlarge the turkey design if you choose. Reproduce the filigree pattern in metal and glue all the sections together. Spray with black or gold paint when glue has hardened and hang on the wall.

DECOUPAGED CANS

*C*ans that originally contained food — coffee, vegetables and fruit — were covered with paper cutouts from an outdated Australian Women's Diary, then découpaged.

Read general instructions for découpage on pages 20-22 before beginning this project. A general materials list for découpage also appears on page 19.

Extra materials
• cans • *methylated spirits* • *lint-free rag* • *metal primer* • *black paint*

Instructions
Thoroughly clean the surface of the cans inside and out with soap and water. Dry. Wipe over the outside with methylated spirits to remove the remaining glue or gum from the label adhesion. Use steel wool if necessary. Rinse in a solution of vinegar and water. Dry.

Apply a coat of metal primer to prevent rust if the cans are not in good condition.

Paint the lid plus upper and lower rims with black paint. Protect with a coat of sealer. Alternatively, leave the metal in its original state.

Proceed as for general instructions for découpage (pages 20-22). Make sure the entire metal surface is covered with paper cutouts, overlapping layers of different shapes to give an interesting collage.

Découpaged cans

RECYCLED
glass

*I*n most homes people throw away a minimum of five glass jars or bottles every week. Fortunately glass can be recycled again and again — used for the same purpose or adapted with a little flair and creativity into something totally new. It is amazing how many craft techniques can be applied to a glass container to give it a new lease of life.

Save different kinds of bottles and jars, building up a collection so that when the opportunity arises to recycle there are plenty of shapes and sizes from which to choose: jam and spice jars, soda, liquor, medicine and wine bottles, as well as small jars of imported jams, relish and baby food. Even ordinary used light globes can be successfully transformed into stunning Christmas decorations.

From the application of paint, paper and florals in quick, easy ways to the more complicated techniques of découpage, marbling, folk art and imitation stained glass, the results will be rewarding and individual.

Usually a good soaking in some hot water is sufficient to remove the labels from the glass. Any residual stickiness can be removed by rubbing with some steel wool; stubborn glue can be removed with methylated spirits. Wash the glass well with detergent, rinse and wash again in vinegar and water. Rinse in hot water. Do not fill internally painted or découpaged glass with water-soluble substances as the finish may lift off.

———

RECYCLED JARS AND BOTTLES

———

Storage jars

- Create pretty storage jars by painting the lids in bright colours to match a colour scheme. Or cover them with circles of fabric cut with pinking shears and tied attractively with ribbon.
- Any-sized wine bottle, once washed and sterilised, is great for storing homemade vinegars and sauces. Just add purchased corks.
- Stick abstract or silhouette shapes from Contact paper onto the glass container.
- Tie a miniature bouquet of fresh or dried flowers or herbs around the neck of the bottle or jar.
- If giving a gift of homemade jam, decorate the container with simple drawings of the appropriate fruits using felt tipped pens, or glue on magazine cutouts.
- Add a decorative scene or character created from air- or oven-dried clay to the lid of baby food jars. Fill with lollies or pot pourri.

———

89

Decorated bottles

- Save clear glass bottles. Clean and dry them thoroughly. Create an interesting effect by swirling two or three different coloured enamel paints around inside the bottle. This will not be waterproof unless sealed accordingly.
- A clear glass milk bottle can be painted internally with white paint then stencilled on the outside surface with blue paint. Add a few dried flowers.
- Attach a fabric cutout to the glass surface with fusible webbing. Outline and add internal design detail with dimensional paint.
- Add vitality to a dull corner by grouping closely together an assortment of bottles painted with enamels in a wide range of colours. Spray cans of iridescent enamels for cars are useful for this purpose. Highlights of a different colour can be added to a thin mono-coloured base coat using stippling, dribbling or sponging.

Fun ideas with recycled glass

Table centres

Romantic table centres can be created by spray painting a wine bottle and adding a candle, or by filling baby food jars with candle wax and decorating the outside surface of the glass.

DÉCOUPAGED GLASS

*I*n this type of découpage the paper cutouts are applied inside or outside a glass container, or underneath a glass plate where, if the background is painted, it takes on the appearance of decorated porcelain.

When the cutouts are placed under or inside the glass, the glass acts as a natural protective coat for the design, making it unnecessary to apply the traditional many layers of varnish.

Read the general instructions for découpage on pages 20-22 before making découpaged glass items. There is also a general materials list for découpage on page 19.

A selection of glass
containers for recycling

Extra Materials
• oil based paint • wallpaper paste (cellulose)
• non-glossy paper cutouts • methylated spirits • glass jars and
containers with a wide enough neck to fit hands into • clear glass plate
• crayon or china marking pencil

Instructions

Prepare the glass as in general instructions on page 89. It is very important for the glass to be perfectly clean, but avoid chemical glass cleaners as some leave a coating that resists the glue. After the final rinse, dry the glass with a lint-free cloth or sheets of newspaper. From this point on the glass should be handled as little as possible so that no new fingerprints, grease or dirt appear.

The preparation of the cutouts and the gluing procedure are the same as for general découpage.

Découpage on top of the glass: The procedures are exactly the same as for general découpage.

Paint the lid in a light colour with acrylic paint. Seal. Add the paper cutouts and treat as on glass.

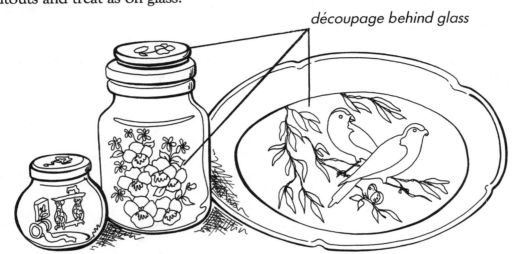

découpage behind glass

découpage on top of glass

Découpage on glass

Découpage behind glass: Never use shiny papers or spray with a sealer. Very thin paper should also be avoided as the background paint tends to show through.

Make a paper pattern the same size as the glass surface to be decorated and arrange the cutouts on that or facing upwards under the glass, secured with Blutack. When satisfied, outline the pieces on the front of glass with a crayon or china marking pencil.

Use a cellulose wallpaper paste to stick the cutouts to the glass. Place paste on the printed face of each piece and press down onto the underside of the glass with damp fingers and a sponge.

Check gluing and remove air bubbles as in general découpage. Hold the glass at an angle and look at the design from the front; any shiny spots visible indicate air bubbles. Work them out as described on page 21. If the cutouts are not glued down totally the paint will seep under the design.
Before putting on the background paint, coat the design with a sealer.

Apply an oil-based background paint over the back of the design and over the glass. Oil paint takes quite a few days to dry. When you have applied two or three coats, the result will look like porcelain.

Sand the surface of the paint smooth.

To finish, apply three to six coats of varnish over the painted surface. The glass item may now be washed by hand.

Or, instead of painting, you can finish with a sheet of special paper such as rice or mulberry paper, then seal and varnish as before.

IMITATION STAINED GLASS

*I*t is hard to believe these storage jars were once rescued from the rubbish. They may look as though they are stained glass but the effect is actually achieved with a bottle of simulated lead adhesive and glass paints. Fill the jars or just place them on a window sill so the sunlight streams through the design.

The basic technique is to outline the design in the lead and colour in with the paint. The leading is what actually holds the paint onto the glass. The cured paint is not waterproof.

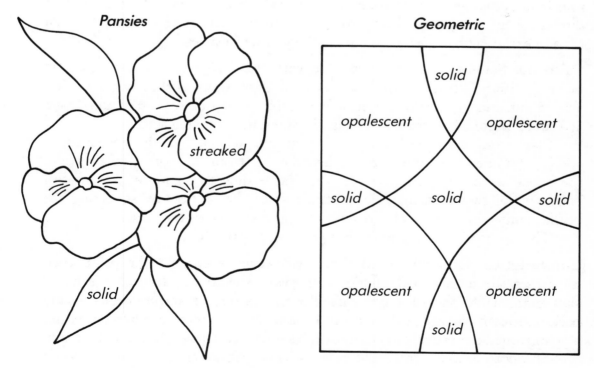

Stained glass patterns

Materials

• used glass jars, cleaned • liquid leading • textured glass paints: green (G), light blue (LB), dark blue (DB), white (W), rose (R), crystal clear (CC) • pattern • paper towelling • damp cloth • sharp craft knife • glass cleaner • toothpicks or timber skewers • sheet of lined paper • mylar plastic sheeting • masking tape • eye dropper

Instructions

Clean the glass surface thoroughly using the cleaner and dry well with the towelling.

Position the traced pattern inside the jar, securing with a strip of tape.

Leading: Create the lead outlining strips on mylar plastic. To help in making these lines straight, place the plastic over a lined sheet of paper. Grip the bottle of leading as you would a broom handle, tap it vertically on a hard surface to bring the leading to the tip and begin to trace over a printed line. Apply an even, continuous pressure to the bottle. Leave overnight to cure, or longer if necessary as the curing is affected by weather conditions.

Peel off a strip of leading. Choose the longest run possible in the pattern and, without stretching, lay the leading onto the glass following these lines. Press the leading down to prevent air or moisture getting to the paint. Strips can be joined together later with extra leading. Intersecting strips should be cut straight at the junction so the leading meets but does not overlap. Each join in the leading must be touched up with a drop of liquid leading applied directly from the bottle. Leave to dry overnight. Use a craft knife to trim off any excess blobs or irregularities in the width of the leading.

Painting: Stabilise the jar on its side with the design area uppermost and begin to paint. Work fast with the textured glass paints as they begin to cure almost immediately after application. Concentrate on one section of the design at a time, beginning in the top left hand corner, then moving across.

Plain areas of the design such as the leaves and a few of the flower petals are first outlined with the paint applied directly from the bottle, making sure the edges are in constant contact with the leading to create an instant seal between the two mediums. Fill in the rest of the section by squeezing the bottle gently while moving it slowly back and forth across the surface.

The paints will appear milky but go clearer as they dry.

Combing: Combing with a toothpick or skewer evens out the paint level, minimises the number of bubbles and gives a realistic texture to the cured glass paint. Hold the stick perpendicular to the surface and move it quickly back and forth through the paint, moving from the top to the bottom either in a horizontal or vertical direction. Comb similar sections in the same direction.

Stubborn bubbles can be removed by sucking them back into the bottle or into an eye dropper.

Special Painting Techniques

Marbled: Put a dot of W onto the centre corner of the petal. Follow this with a line of DB. Fill in the rest of the petal in LB. With a clean toothpick move the W paint through the DB into the LB in a feathery fashion. Clean the toothpick after each stroke through the paints so the colours do not become muddy.

Opalescent: Place scattered dots of one colour over a section. Fill in the surrounding area with a second colour. Using a toothpick, swirl the two colours together. 'Less rather than more' is applicable for the amount of mixing required.

Cathedral: This technique creates a uniform bumpy appearance using CC. Apply paint as in the general instructions but move the bottle from side to side and up and down over the glass to create the texture.

RECYCLED LIGHT GLOBES

*M*ost people, when they replace a light globe, simply throw the old one out without thinking. But these blown globes can be transformed into wonderful Christmas decorations by painting on patterns of comma strokes using metallic acrylics or by marbling with glass enamel paints. Search out some of the more unusual globe shapes to add variety.

Painted Christmas decorations

Materials
• *assorted light globes* • *acrylic sealer* • *metallic acrylic paints — pure gold (PG), royal red (RR), blue topaz (BT), aquamarine (A), amethyst (AM)* • *sea sponge* • *paper towelling* • *No. 3 round brush* • *white palette* • *3 m (3½ yds) of 3 mm (¹/₁₀") wide ribbon in co-ordinated colours* • *craft glue* • *high gloss varnish* • *brush to apply varnish* • *mineral turpentine to clean brush*

Instructions

Clean the globes as for glass in general. Spray each globe with sealer and allow to dry.

Paint the globe attachment at the top PG.

Squeeze one of the background colours onto the palette. Dip the sponge into this colour then pounce lightly onto paper towelling to remove the excess paint. Next pounce the sponge all over the surface of the globe. On some globes try applying several colours for a mottled effect. Leave to dry.

The design is based on a comma stroke which can be angled left or right. Fill the brush three-quarters full of paint. Place the brush to the surface, press the bristles down gently so they fan out while keeping the handle vertical. Pull and lift slowly as the brush is dragged slowly in direction required. The bristles will return to form a point at the end of the stroke.

Complete freehand comma strokes, varying the length and direction according to the design chosen. Two designs are shown, one for round globes and one for long globes. Add dots where indicated.

While the globes are drying, store them in a homemade container: punch holes in an egg carton and insert the already painted attachments into these holes.

When dry, brush on a coat of gloss varnish. Leave to dry overnight. Wash brush in mineral turpentine.

Cut ribbons to lengths of 50 cm (20″) each.

Apply glue to the globe attachments. Tie two or three different coloured ribbon lengths around the attachment and finish in a bow.

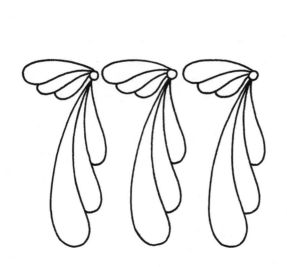

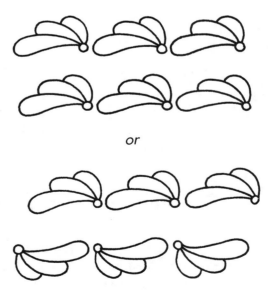

or

long globes

round globes

Patterns for light globes

Marbled light globes

In this technique, acrylic paint is floated on the surface of a liquid. Swirled or combed patterns are made, then transferred to the glass globes.

Materials

• *Liquitex Glossies acrylic enamels* • *light globes* • *3 mm (¹/₁₀″) wide ribbon* • *deep container for immersing* • *Marble Magic powder* • *timber skewers* • *homemade stand for drying globes* • *rubber gloves* • *paper towelling* • *newspaper* • *gloss varnish* • *brush to apply varnish* • *craft glue*

Instructions

Prepare the marbling solution the night before required. Measure the quantity of water to three-quarters fill the container. Add this amount of warm water and sprinkle the correct proportion of Marble Magic over the surface. Overnight the powder will change to a gel which must then be stirred through the water giving a clear, thick solution with a slippery feel.

Break skewers in half and use these to stir up the paints. Dilute each colour with a little water so the paints can be dropped from the stirring sticks onto the surface of the thick solution. Each drop of paint will float on the surface, slowly spreading to form a circle. Add no more than three colours.

Using the pointed end of a clean skewer, push, pull, swirl or drag the circles of paint into intricate patterns. Do not hurry and do not overwork the design — the simplest pattern is often the most effective. The marbling solution keeps the colours from merging together, making possible these marvellous patterns.

Wearing rubber gloves, carefully lower the globe horizontally through the patterned surface until completely immersed. The globe will collect the colour as it passes through. Lift it quickly so it will not be marbled twice.

Place each marbled globe in the stand to dry. When dry place in a preheated oven at 325° F (160° C) for 30 to 40 minutes to cure.

Decorate with ribbons as for decorative painted globes.

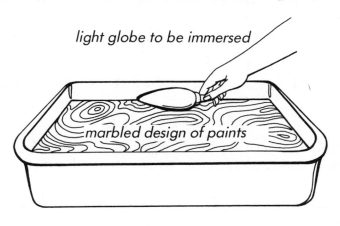

light globe to be immersed

marbled design of paints

Marbling on glass

Recycled paper

- Additional reading:
  Papermaking — From Recycling to Art by Jean G. Kropper, Lothian.
  Jean also offers classes in paper making and undertakes commissions for her original artwork. Phone: (02) 427 7612.
  Découpage — An Illustrated Guide by Nerida Singleton, Sally Milner Publishing.
  Découpage — A Guide to the Creative Art Form by Audrey Raymond (a member of the National Guild of Découpeurs, America), Simon & Schuster.
- Extra samples for photography kindly supplied by Amanda Ho — chest, briefcase, small case, hexagonal box and jewellery; Audrey Raymond — vase, small door knobs, ivory container with lid, door finger plates; Judy Poulos — large door knobs; Dorothy White — tray, cream container with lid.
- Papermaking kit: Papermakers Paper Recycling Kit, New Zealand (0014 800 128 925) free phone.

Recycled fabric

- The linen bear, silk tie photo album and picture frame were designed and made by Denise Lawler. Denise works from her shop 'Cottage Crafts' at Camden. Phone: (046) 55 7071.
- The beautiful christening set was designed and made by Glenda Overstead.
- Lyn Inall, a respected teacher of patchwork and quilting, designed and made the bears and pillows from recycled denim. Phone: (062) 88 3497.
- The teddy bears are based on McCall's Crafts pattern 2629 and Dream Spinners Bittersweet Bear pattern 114 by Great American Quilt Factory, Inc.
- The Blooming Cushion is based on a technique from the Bloomin' Vest™ pattern by The Cambio.

Recycled bric a brac

- Sandra Flannery and her daughter Debbie created the distinctive junk wall hangings. Both accept commissions. Phone: (066) 76 6317.
- The spectacle lenses were painted by Lorell McIntyre.
- Susie Pullen from Silk Road provided the silks and dyes for the button projects. Phone: (043) 67 6449.

Recycled cans

- Anne Colligan designed and painted on the assortment of cans.

Recycled glass

- Glass plate for photography was découpaged by Lorraine Millar.
- Lorell McIntyre designed and completed the decorative painting on the light globes.
- DMC/Myart supplied the liquid leading and stained glass paints. Phone: (02) 559 3088.
- Binney & Smith supplied the Liquitex paints. Phone: (03) 560 5633.